Finding The One
How Dating Prepares You For Marriage

By
Christian Dunn

Elany Arts Publishing

ISBN: 978-0-6151-4546-4

Elany Arts, Inc
website: http://www.elanyarts.com

To my wife, Mandy—

Without you this book would not have been possible on so many levels. Thank you for your constant love, support, and encouragement, and for believing in this book (and in me) even when I didn't.

It has been over 10 years since we first started dating. We have been through so much together since then—so many amazing life-changing experiences, and some truly heart breaking ones as well. Reflecting on these experiences, all I can think is how grateful I am that I got to go through them all—good and bad—with you. I do not know how I could have made it to here without you.

You are a constant source of strength, grace, and inspiration and I love you dearly.

Table of Contents

Acknowledgements

All of these people have helped me in so many ways, without them this book would not be what it is today. Thank you!

My Parents—For always believing in me and showing me unconditional love; you have taught me more than you know. For making me feel like I could do whatever I set out to do.

Elany Arts—For everything! For supporting my family and me in so many ways, for being a blessing in many people's lives, for believing in this book and making it become a reality!

Jonathan and Rebekah—For your constant love and support, for refining my ideas as iron sharpens iron, and for getting me to call Mandy those many years ago!

Jason and Darby—For pushing me to keep going when I was ready to give up on this book, for being there for Mandy and me "in the beginning," for always believing.

Joe and Mindy—For constantly supporting me, for being friends we can count on in good times and bad, and for challenging me to make this book the best it can be.

Collin and Lindsay—For standing by our side no matter what, and for your friendship and love.

Bruce and Lynn—For your rare example of a lasting and strong marriage that we were able to look up to as a young couple, and still do. For your many hours of advice and revisions—thank you!

Rob—For challenging me to expect a lot from myself and to dream bigger dreams. For believing all those years ago when I started, that I could actually write a book!

Chad and Chrissy—For all the memories we have shared, and will share. For the privilege of being part of a family with you.

Heather and Alex—For your love and friendship over the years. You have been a great source of encouragement for me.

Charky, Laurie, and Nanny—For your friendship and support. I am so blessed to be part of your family!

My Friends—There are so many more I would love to thank. So many of you have taught me so much through your encouragement over the years, and your examples of faith and love. I cherish you all.

My Youth Group—For your honest (even brutal!) advice about this book, and for still thinking it was worthwhile. You guys are awesome!

My Wife and Kids—For being the greatest gifts in my life. I never knew I could love, and be loved, with such depth and joy. I am truly blessed.

My God—For being with me through it all—You've never left my side. You are the source of everything I cherish and I am truly grateful.

Foreword

I have been asked the same questions. Dating or courting? How will I know if he's 'The One'? How far is too far? How will I ever trust someone again? Why not me?

As a pastor of young people for 25 years, and the father of three teenagers, I recognize these questions and realize that they're not going away They remain important because relationships are important. But they remain persistent for a number of reasons. They're persistent because our culture offers so many disparate answers; few of which reference, and many of which flaunt, biblical wisdom. They're persistent because faithful teachers have vast differences about how to apply biblical wisdom to the topic of dating. And they're persistent because dating, as we know it, was not an ancient practice. Abraham sent his servant to find a wife for his son. The servant accomplished the task by praying and watching for a young woman with a heart for thirsty camels. We have, by and large, moved to a different model of finding a spouse.

In response to these important and persistent questions, my friend Christian Dunn has written this helpful book. Christian has answered these questions and others with a pastor's heart, a practitioner's wisdom and desire to apply faithfully the teaching of scripture to the confused romantic landscape of the church. I commend to you his work, and plan to share it with my teenagers as well.

Mark Tindall, pastor
Blue Route Vineyard, Media, PA

Introduction

Humble Beginnings

Writing a book about dating can feel a bit like splashing to make waves in the ocean. When I first began working on this, I walked into a local Christian bookstore to peruse the existing books on dating. I was struck (and somewhat discouraged) by the volume and variety of works already on the shelf. What could I possibly have to add? But over the past 10 years of my life I have become convinced that teens and young adults are still searching for leadership in the area of dating. So this book is my attempt at a "wave."

One thing I noticed about the other "waves" was that most of the author's names ended in "Ph.D." This is not the case with me. I have not studied relationships extensively, I do not have a Ph.D. or even a Masters, and I have never published a book before. So, my heart in writing this book is not to claim to have all the answers or to be an expert in this field. What I plan to offer, though, is a unique perspective and practical, down to earth advice that will help you.

Over the past 10 years I have had the joy of serving God through ministry to teens and young adults. At 16 years old I began leading a small group in my house with a friend. When I was 18 the group of twelve had grown into a group of over 50 teens with a desire to know God. At this time we began hosting meetings to encourage other teens to "catch on fire" for God. Out of this grew something we called "East Coast Aflame." ECA started as a lone youth conference in the fall of 1996. As a result of this conference, we received invitations to hold similar conferences in over 11 states in the Northeast and Northwest of the US. Through these experiences I have had the opportunity to minister to literally thousands of young people, and to talk to hundreds of teens and young adults specifically about dating and marriage. Over the past decade I have noticed a growing trend in my conversations.

People in my generation are having a hard time understanding God's will in their lives for dating and marriage. Does God approve of dating? Is dating sinful? How do I know when I've "found the one?" Fueling these questions is a growing pressure in our current Christian culture to only date one person your whole life—implying that the first person you date will be your spouse. This pressure is creating problems for teens and young adults that I feel are unfair and dangerous. This book is meant to bring understanding about where this pressure is coming from, and guidance on how to navigate dating relationships in a Godly and healthy way.

Since I began writing, I have taught this material several times, and shared much of it with individuals who have come to me for counsel and advice. Through this process, my ideas have been refined and sometimes altered. But most of all, these experiences have solidified my conviction that another "wave" is needed. Even with all the existing books on dating, people are still searching for guidance. I am not claiming that this book will be *the* answer but I hope it will provide *some* answers to many who read it. I have a passion to see people in my generation learn how to enter into dating relationships in a healthy and Godly manner, as well as establish strong and happy marriages that will last.

Welcome to My Office

I thought for a long time about what "voice" I should write this book in. I wondered at the outset whether I should sound academic, or religious, or preachy, or colloquial. What I have decided is to write as if I were talking to you in my office because you had come to me seeking pastoral guidance. So as you begin to read this book, imagine yourself, either on your own or as a couple, coming into my office and asking me questions about love, dating, relationships, marriage, and how to find direction in all of those. Imagine it being a very informal setting. This is not a high-pressure meeting; I am not trying to force my opinions on you in any way. We are just hanging out together, talking about Jesus and His plans in your life. Approach this book that way, reading it as if I were talking to you right there.

As you read the book, know that I am just sharing from my heart, my experiences, and my understanding of how Biblical truth applies to all these situations. And then take what I have said and pray over it. Take it to people you trust and test it. Ask the Lord to show you what of my advice is good for you. My hope is that God will use this book to refine you, make you fall more in love with him, and gain greater peace in the direction you are taking in your life.

Another thing you should know before starting this book is that I use many stories from people I have met over the past few years. Most stories are very generally referenced, and for those that are specifically recounted, I have obtained permission from those involved. All names have been changed.

Lastly, I know that in writing a book, I can't control who reads it. People of any age can pick this up and begin reading it. So, for clarity's sake I want to just give some instructions to three major age groups I anticipate reading this—young teens, older teens and young adults, and parents.

Attention Young Teens!

When I was 14 years old, I had a friend who literally read every book on dating that he could find. The two of us would spend hours talking about our thoughts and beliefs on the subject. I know that young people from 11-15 years old seriously think about this topic, and that many begin to experiment with "romantic" relationships of one kind or another. What I want to say to young teens that are under 16 years old is that first of all, you need to get your parents involved in your decisions about dating. I know this sounds very strange to some of you, but your parents do have your best interests at heart. For those of you who simply can't talk to your parents, I strongly encourage you to talk to a youth pastor or pastor and allow them to speak into your life.

As far as my book is concerned, you need to understand that even if your parents feel you are too young to date there is still much for you to learn in here. In fact, before you ever start dating is a great time to read this as it will prepare you for what you will someday encounter. I honestly think that there is an age that is "too young" to date. I don't think that it is the same age for every teenager though. I think that it can vary depending on the maturity of the individual plus many other factors. So, if you are 12 or 13 please don't read this book and go tell your parents that I am saying you should start dating! This book argues that dating is not inherently evil and that there is a Godly way to date. But if you are too young, then you need to wait until you are ready. The book of Song of Solomon tells us not to awaken love before it is ready—be careful—you do not want to start dating before you are ready. Listen to your parents. Listen to your youth pastor and pastor. And listen to God. They will lead you, and release you when you are ready, but don't be in a rush. God's timing is always best.

For Older Teens and Young Adults

For those of you reading this book who are older teens (16 and older) and young adults (20 and older) I strongly encourage you to get your parents' advice and input on dating and relationships. Along with that, I pray that this book can be a guide for you as you navigate the relationships that God brings into your life. The older you get, the more you are going to think about "finding the one" and moving into that next stage of your life. I wrote this book for you who are wondering about dating. Some of you might have heard many messages about dating being wrong, and hopefully this book will help to bring some balance to your perspective. Some of you may have never heard any negative messages about dating, and wonder what all the hype is about. I still encourage you to read this book because the majority of this book is aimed at helping young Christians create and sustain healthy and Godly dating relationships.

A Message To The Parents

Finally, I want to make a quick note to the parents. I know that in writing a book on dating, it is inevitable that many teens will pick this up in hopes of finding a Christian author with liberal views on dating. I think it is important for you, as the parent, to understand that I totally and fully support your authority in your child's life. It is important for your children to know this too. I know that even some parents in my own church will not agree with some of what I have written in this book. And it is crucial for you to know that if you do not agree with what I write, please communicate to your child that your word comes first. I am writing this book to a large audience; it is impossible to anticipate every parent's guidelines for dating.

I encourage you to also read this book if your child is reading it. And then talk to them about it. Ask them what they think about it. Use this book as a catalyst to open up discussion in an area where children desperately need their parents. The greatest influences in my life in my early dating years were definitely my parents, and I felt I could share anything with them. I encourage you to listen without judgment, and offer advice in humility. Let them know you do not have all the answers either, and work with them as you develop guidelines and rules to protect and safeguard them. I am a young parent, but I am already beginning to see the awesomeness of this responsibility. Be blessed as you continue to guide your child.

In summary, parents: Get involved. My generation is often leaderless, and therefore easily misguided. They need you, and want you to be a parent in their life. So do it. It is your God-given gift and role, and they need you to fill that place in their lives. And to those of you who are reading this book for guidance: Do so prayerfully. I encourage you to open your mind and heart to what I have to say, and ask God to show you how this all applies to your life.

Small Group Discussion Questions
One of my goals in writing this book was to help teens start thinking and talking in more open and healthy ways about this topic. One great way to foster this is through small groups. To this end, I have included several small group discussion questions at the end of each chapter. If you are not in a group right now, you can use these questions to further your personal growth as an individual. If you are in a group, use them to generate discussions that will challenge your thinking on dating and expand your heart for God. These questions are only meant to be a launching pad. Make more of your own if you like! You can also download the Finding The One Small Group Leader's Manual to assist in leading these small groups at www.christianjdunn.com.

What are we listening to?

Exposing the dangers of the culture of pressure

About two years ago I was meeting regularly with a young man named Alan (age 17) about dealing with issues in life, getting closer to God, and staying accountable. I had known for about two months that he was starting to have interest in this one particular girl, and I was watching to see how he would handle the situation. One day, Alan came in for our time together, and sat down in the chair very exasperated. He needed help. The question he asked floored me. He said essentially, "I have been praying really seriously about Megan—she is on my mind a lot, and we have been talking on the phone some. I have been praying, because I want to know from God if she is the one or not. I do not want to date her, or go any further in our relationship, before knowing if she is the one—and she feels the same way. So we are praying and trying to find out if we are supposed to get married eventually. I have been talking to my parents about it too—but I want to ask you, how did you know that Mandy (my wife) was the one? What should I do to figure this out?"

My reaction then, as it is every time this situation happens to me, was "What! Why are you talking about marriage now? You barely know each other!" Let me ask you a question—do you think marriage is an important decision? How important? I would argue that it is the single most important decision of your life (outside of accepting Christ as your Savior). One that (if you are a Christian) cannot be reversed or changed except in extreme cases. So, if it is this monumental, life-altering decision, why are youngsters across America trying to make this decision when they barely know each other—before they have even been on a date—before they have ever had a single disagreement? The reason is that we, as American Christians, are living in a culture of pressure.

The Culture of Pressure

As I mentioned in the introduction, since 1994 I have been leading a meeting for youth and young adults every week. Since 1996 I have co-led a ministry that holds conferences and training schools encouraging teens and young adults to radically commit their lives to Christ. I have spoken to thousands of young people, and individually prayed with, counseled, and advised hundreds.

I say all of that to say this—both locally and abroad, I have seen a new kind of "dating pressure." There is a palpable pressure on teens and young adults to abide by a new set of rules for dating and finding their mate. I believe that these rules are the Church's attempt to protect young people from how dating is portrayed in secular culture. However, young people tell me that these rules are bringing more bondage than freedom, more confusion than guidance, and more unhealthy relationships than Godly ones.

Let me give you an example of what I have been hearing from young people about this pressure:

> Teens and young adults—you should refrain from dating
> all together. Dating leads to many sinful things: it is almost
> impossible to date without sinning. Instead, you need to
> wait to date until you find "the one" you are going to marry.
> If you date someone who is not your eventual spouse you
> are wasting yourself, and you are betraying your spouse. To
> sum it up—you should only date one person your whole
> life—your wife or husband.

Sounds like the kind of pressure you want to be out there, right? It is certainly better that Christian youth are abstaining from dating all together than being sexually promiscuous—who could argue with that? It also sounds amazingly romantic, even ideal, to only date one person your whole life, get married, have kids (can you hear the violins playing?) and live happily ever after. Why is this a bad thing?

It is bad because it is avoidance rather than intentional involvement.

If the best advice we can give our young people about dating is to not date, how are we helping them? Moreover, as many of our youth attempt to live out this ideology, they are suffering consequences. If the Church does not find a more balanced understanding of how relationships develop and a more healthy way of finding our spouses, then our generation could be plagued with the same divorce rate as our parents' generation, or we will all stay single, paralyzed by fear. I honor the intentions behind this new wave of ideology in the church, protecting young people from the world, and teaching us the power of covenant relationships. However, in an effort to shield us from the world, an equally dangerous environment has been created.

How can I say that? Because I have seen the negative effects already, and most of our generation is not old enough to see the effects this pressure will produce later in marriage. Free will is one of the greatest, most powerful gifts that God ever gave to humans. It is so powerful because it is the one way in which we can be total individuals, even to the fault of individualizing, or separating ourselves from our own Creator. That power in humans is unthinkable, yet God honored and loved us enough to trust us with it. As a loving Father he gave us the chance to use our free will for good or evil.

Now it seems in this culture of isolation from, and fear of the world, that the Modern Christian culture is attempting to usurp our young peoples' free wills. We are telling them they can have only one choice, one chance, and then pressuring them to stay with that. We are taking away the right to change their minds. We are telling them there is no possibility for them to grow and find that maybe God intended a different person to marry. We are setting up an expectation that for most people is unrealistic.

In the rest of this chapter I will discuss four problems that arise from the pressure being put on young adults to only date one person, and have that person be their spouse. The four problems are: 1) Being paralyzed by the fear of making a mistake, 2) Having difficulty starting relationships, 3) Breaking up becoming a failure, and 4) Marrying the wrong person for the wrong reasons. As you read through these problems, think of them as symptoms. These are symptoms of the pressure young adults are feeling. These are signs of what this pressure is doing to young adults. Also, as you read these, think about whether you (or someone you know) have ever experienced any of these. If so, can you see the pressure in your life that I have described?

Problem #1
Being Paralyzed By the Fear of Making a Mistake
I have a good friend who is around twenty—two years old and leads a very
large ministry to young people. I respect his thoughts a lot, so I told him
that I was writing this book and asked him what question about dating he
wish he knew the answer to. This is a young man who is already in a very
prominent leadership role in the church—this is the church's leadership of
tomorrow, and this is how the Modern Christian culture is preparing him—
he said: "I just wish I knew why it is so wrong for me to go out alone with
a girl just as friends. Just to get something to eat. Why can't I find someone
who doesn't want to figure out marriage on the first date?"

Can you believe that? Maybe I am the only person in the nation who
thinks this is amazing, but to hear one of the more mature Christians in my
generation saying that makes me cringe with the thoughts of where others
must be! Think of the pressure this guy must be feeling for that to be the
most pressing question on his mind about dating. He didn't ask, "How do
I know if I'm in love?" or "How long should we date?" or "Give me some
advice on how to treat a girl that I'm dating." No it was—"Why can't I find
someone who doesn't want to figure out marriage on the first date?" What
have we created?

The desire to not date, or simply the inability to date because you
cannot figure out how, is definitely a symptom of this pressure. Think about
it—if you were given this assignment, how would you respond: Go out and
make friends with girls—take your time, but pray and ask God to show you
which of these girls you should marry. You can't take them on a date; you
can only be friends. So try to figure this out, and remember—you only have
one chance at this, because after you start dating . . .. you can never go back!

My response would be the same as my friend's—forget dating
all together! This pressure is so intense that it paralyzes many from even
wanting to deal with male/female relationships. Many would rather forget
about the whole thing, or wait until God himself appears and tells them
whom to marry, than to get out there and find a spouse.

Maybe the worst part of this is that it makes no sense! What is so
bad about dating? Echoing what my friend said—why is it bad for him to go
out with a girl just for fun, just to get to know each other? Why is it wrong
(watch out, I am about to get really radical) to date someone, and then not
marry her! (gasp!) Who found that verse in the Bible? What is so evil and
against God's will about two mature Christians dating, and then breaking
up? Why do we insist that is bad—is it possible that could even be good?

What is inherently sinful with breaking up? In fact—one could argue that God could even tell you to date someone whom you are not going to marry—for the mere reason that he is going to use that relationship to prepare both of you for your spouses!

Is everyone OK? Are you still reading? I know that was a little radical. Obviously I am being sarcastic and having some fun here, but I am trying to make a point. The point is, after seeing so many of my peers crippled by this pressure, I have come to completely and totally disagree with the principles upon which the pressure is founded. I see no proof for them in the Scriptures and I see a lot of negative fruit. I simply do not see the inherent evil and danger in dating that other people seem to see. I agree there is, of course, opportunity to sin, but show me one situation in the world where that opportunity does not exist! James teaches us that we are led away "by our own evil desires." You do not need a dating relationship for that to happen; sin happens anywhere there is a willing soul.

So why single out dating? Because of the chance of sex? My response to this is a little harsh too, sorry, but the church needs to give Christian teens a little more respect! "Train your children in the way they should go"—we are not called to dictate where they will go, but to trust them to be able to put their "training" into practice. As a church we need to focus on leading our kids into real, relevant, and powerful relationships with Jesus, so that they learn to resist sin and submit to God on their own. Simply shielding them from the world, and hiding them from the opportunity to sin, does nothing but weaken them.

Being involved in youth ministry at several levels for a couple of years, I have noticed a trend—the church is slowly learning how to empower their youth, rather than simply entertain them or set them aside. This is very good, but we need to, as a church, get into the game as far as dating is concerned. Sometimes I feel that Modern Christianity uses fear tactics or peer pressure to keep the next generation from dating, because we are too afraid of the power and seduction of the world. However, we need to be doing just the opposite. The Church needs to have the answers for our teens and young adults. Rather than just telling them not to date, we need to address the issues and problems that are being faced by our generation. We need to invest, to teach, to mentor, and to lead—just as Jesus did.

If the Church does not give the answers, then the world certainly will. So we need to trust our kids. I am not saying we should not put boundaries on them, that is ridiculous—God certainly puts boundaries on us. But we should train them, teach them, give them healthy boundaries, and then help them to go forward into the world and make good decisions for themselves!

Instead of people in my generation feeling secure, confident, and strong in their quest for their life partners, many are running and hiding. Instead of feeling empowered to discern God's will for our lives, we are entering into the greatest decision of our lives paralyzed by the fear of making a mistake. This is clearly not God's will for us. The Lord calls us to have a "sound mind" not a "spirit of fear" (2 Timothy 1:7, NKJV) and to be renewed in His power so that we can test and approve what the "will of God" is (Romans 12:2). This culture of pressure being perpetuated by Modern Christianity is, instead of directing my generation to these scriptures, placing my generation in a bondage of fear—fear of never finding "the one," fear of breaking up, and fear of choosing the wrong person.

We need to change the culture in which we live. We need to take a fresh look at dating. If I can just get you to look at dating with new glasses, and consider the possibility that we have overreacted, that maybe dating is not from Satan himself, that maybe God uses it in our lives—then I will be very happy. If Modern Christianity can move towards a culture of freedom and trust and true Godly guidance, rather than using fear to avoid the difficulties dating does create—we will see much healthier relationships.

Problem #2
Having Difficulty Starting Relationships
I have another friend named Chloe who recently sent me an email. Chloe is 19 and has never had a boyfriend. She wrote me because she has a good guy friend, and was wondering if she should stop or cut back, their relationship. She did not know for sure if he was the one for her—she knew that they got along great, and that he was a very good Christian, but she just did not know if they were meant to be. Her fear was that if they continued to remain close friends, that she would soon begin to have "more than friendship feelings" for him. Then she would be in big trouble because she would still not know if he was the one, and then what would she do?

Do you see the problem here? This is so unhealthy! A 19 year old girl, who is a very mature Christian, feels guilty about being friends with a wonderful Christian boy because maybe she might start to like him! Again I ask my question—why is that bad? This is the second symptom or problem arising because of this pressure that our generation feels—an extreme difficulty in starting a relationship. In Chloe's case she is not even close to starting a relationship, she is having difficulty just having male friends! What is happening to my generation because of this pressure is so sad. Sometimes I just want to grab people who tell me these things and say—"Chill out! Calm down! He is just a boy—you are just a girl—be friends! If you start liking him, its not the end of the world—in fact you might find that God approves ....wow! Imagine that!" After explaining to Chloe that she truly did not have to figure everything out right away, and that she could date without being totally sure he is the one, her response was "Wow, that takes a lot of pressure off the whole process!" She actually wrote me later again to thank me saying she felt so much less pressure in her relationships and life. She was more confident that God would lead her in his timing and that she could enjoy this relationship. And I have no fear at all that in a couple of months I am going to find that she is sinning horribly, or falling from God, or even drifting into lukewarmness. Her Christianity is intact and she will grow in or out of this relationship based on God's guidance.

That brings me to something else I should address. One argument that people use to discourage young people from dating is that "it will distract you from your relationship with Jesus." A girl at one of our training schools said this to me once, and my reply to her was—"if any relationship distracts you from Jesus, then should you be in it?" The clear answer is no. I agree there are bad dating relationships, but simply because some are bad does not mean all are bad. I had a prayer I used to pray before I met Mandy—that my eventual wife and I would amplify each other's relationships with God and callings from God. Each of us would be better Christians because of the relationship. This is really what we all should be looking for—if any relationship pulls you from Jesus, that is a sure sign to bring it to an end. But to forego all dating based on a fear that it will distract you from Jesus is to come at it the wrong way. The idea that dating will always distract you from Jesus is completely false. If that were true then how would any marriages ever work? If you argue that marriage is different, then are you saying that dating is in and of itself bad? I simply do not see any proof or reason for that. There are bad ones out there—but that does not preclude the existence of great relationships that make people better Christians .... even if they break up in the end!

Getting back to the idea of starting relationships, I believe that relationships—especially romantic and committed ones—need to be created in an environment of peace and not pressure. The current climate makes it difficult for young people to start relationships because they are trying to answer questions that they simply should not be asking yet. Is this my wife/husband? Are we meant to be together forever? Is this the one for me? These are all questions to be answered by couples who have known each other over long periods of time, through good and bad times, in an exclusive and committed relationship, with wise counsel from friends and mentors, and with God's guidance. People who have only been friends for several months, not committed to each other exclusively, should not try to answer these questions.

Asking these questions too early is equivalent to trying to harvest a crop, just days after the seed has gone into the ground. No farmer is upset when there is no visible harvest just days after the seed has been sown. That would be crazy! Every farmer knows it takes time. Time for the seed to grow roots. Time for the seed to grow into the plant it is supposed to be. And more time for this plant to come to maturity and produce fruit. If the farmer were to try and harvest the crop too early, he would end up killing it! This is a good analogy for relationships. If the "M" word comes up too early (marriage, that is)—or if the couple tries to figure out the rest of their lives too quickly—they can often abort the growth of their relationship and it will die before they ever get to see what it could have been.

Some will say that is a good thing. Some will say that this stops bad relationships from starting, and saves ourselves the pain of breaking up, risking sin, and being with someone other than our spouse. I disagree. For most people it is not possible to know if someone is "the one" without having spent a long time in a committed relationship. Therefore you are not saving yourself, you are just answering a question before you could possibly even know the answer and thus stopping all chances of something happening. It is ridiculous, except in the rare case, to expect God to reveal the whole future of your relationship all at once, at the very beginning. God expects us to be involved in the decision. He wants us to get to know each other, to grow together, to find out the likes and dislikes of each other. He wants us to use our God-given minds to discern what his will is. I have seen people take two years to make a decision about college; why are we trying to force people to make marriage decisions so hastily?

Another reason most people cannot know the answers to these questions right up front is that, in the beginning, relationships are not realistic. A friendship alone, for example, is not a realistic environment in which to make decisions about marriage. Excuse the obviously shallow analogy, but when shopping for cars, what do you look at—cars, right? You do not go to the grocery store and try out grocery carts, do you? In the same way, in making the most important decision of your life, you should be looking in the right place. So what is marriage? It is a life-long, committed, romantic, loving, exclusive relationship between two people. So where should you look? In what kind of relationship are you best going to be able to discover if this person is your spouse? The answer is not simply friendship. We need to allow our relationship to escalate into an exclusive, committed, romantic relationship for there to be an honest environment in which to make this judgment. Just as you don't shop for cars at grocery stores, you should not be looking for a life mate in non-committed, non-romantic, non-exclusive friendships! All three of these aspects bring a special change, a certain power to the relationship that no friendship can bring. And when you enter into a relationship like that you are tested, your feelings are tested, and your thoughts are tested in a realistic type of relationship that is relevant and similar to marriage. That is just simple common sense.

Behind all of this there is a huge debate about free will versus predestination. My reasoning thus far relies pretty heavily on free will. I am talking a lot about how the pressure of the Modern Christian culture is effecting how we make our decisions about dating. So I am putting a large emphasis on our part of making the decision for our life partner. A lot of people would say—"it really should not matter, because God will bring the right person at the right time, and you will both know because he is Sovereign." This is a huge theological division in the church ... should I even deal with this?

I do not want to delve too deeply into this, and I certainly do not have all the answers—but let me simply say this. Yes, God is Sovereign. And he is directing and guiding us towards our eventual spouses. But somehow, within his great Will (and this is a mystery) we seem to have some part to play. And so, since I certainly would not dare write a book telling God how to do his part (ha!) I am writing a book trying to help us do a better job on our end. Does that make sense? Since I am writing this for us, most of my reasoning will sound very "free will."

Alright, that is over and I just bored many of you, but I think I needed to get that into the open. To close out this specific section, I just want to say that in order to have healthy, Godly, marital relationships, we need to start with healthy, Godly dating/courting relationships—and these simply cannot be started in the culture of pressure we are living in now. Of the symptoms or problems that I will address, this is both the worst and the most often seen. Almost every one of you that I talk to about dating recognizes this pressure at the outset of relationships. And you go through so much difficulty, so much stress, so much agonizing, worry, and doubt—when your relationship is just in the first stages of growth, and needs to be allowed to grow. You are being forced to start your relationships at level 10 rather than level 1. I want to let you know that it is OK to start at the beginning. Stop forcing yourselves to start at the finish line and work backwards. Take your time to find peace. Enjoy a growing friendship, even when it becomes romantic, without making it too serious too fast. Many people my age have questions about how to do this and another goal of this book is to answer some of these questions.

Problem #3
Breaking Up is Seen as a Failure
If the beginning of relationships is made more difficult by this culture of pressure, then the endings are made almost unbearable. I know someone who follows the theory that he should only date one person, and she should be his wife. Several years ago he felt he had found this person, and began to give his heart, and make plans for the future. However one day, the relationship came to an end. There was nothing he could do to make it go on, it was out of his hands. Now, to me, this story so far is fairly normal—people break up, it hurts, but it happens. Where the story becomes so telling about the culture we live in today is after their breakup.

I watched my friend go into a deep turmoil after this relationship was ended. One main question that haunted him was, had he lost "the one" he was meant to be with? Had he blown it? What if she was it, and now he had missed it? Despair, literally, set in as he contemplated never dating anyone else again. Once this stage of his grief had subsided some, new fears arose—the fears that maybe he had dated the wrong person, and had somehow taken something from the girl whom he would eventually marry! Guilt and shame attacked his thoughts, feeling that he had done something to harm his future wife. He even questioned his ability to hear God's voice. Where was God in this? If God wanted him to marry only one person—then why this? Had he misheard God when he felt the go-ahead to start courting her? Watching my friend go through this made me so angry. Much of his pain was very understandable because he had given over so much of his heart to her. However, I feel that the rising pressure in our culture affected a lot of his thinking and prolonged and accentuated the pain that would normally exist.

There are three major misconceptions that affected the thinking that my friend went through after breaking up. We are taught that 1) the first person you think is the one, must be the one, 2) God would never tell you to date someone he knows is not your eventual spouse, and 3) you are betraying your spouse by dating. These three incorrect ways of viewing dating relationships drive people to despair, guilt, and shame. They tell people that they have failed if their relationship ends in a break up. They tell them that they have hurt their eventual spouse. They tell them that they are out of God's will.

It saddens me to think that the Christian culture of today perpetuates this thinking rather than standing against it with God's truth, but I hear it over and over again in Christian circles. Depending on where you are coming from in your own understanding of dating, some of what I have said has already been radical—but what I am about to write seems (when I share it with others) to be even more so. I want to challenge each of these misconceptions and give you a different way to view them. I want to restate that I do not have all the answers—but I want to shake up our thinking, and challenge us to re-evaluate how we handle dating as Christians.

Misconception #1
The First Person You Think is the One—Must Be the One!
Several summers ago while riding in a van with students from our training school, a few of the students began arguing with my co-leader and me about how they would know they had found "the one." They felt strongly that God had set aside one, and only one, person for them to marry. And now they were waiting until God brought them together. They knew that the first person they got together with would have to be the one. That sounds so romantic, doesn't it? But there are problems with this view.

God knows who you will marry, and if you are obedient to his will in your lives, he will draw you two together. Mandy was born in Idaho, I was born in New York, and we fell in love in Delaware! Clearly God's hand was involved in our relationship. I also prayed for her for years before I even knew that she was the one I would marry. I prayed for my wife, and I truly believe that whole time my prayers were touching her life. The problem with this view is that people take it too far.

Some people feel that since God is bringing you together, you need to just wait and see God do it. This promotes a very stagnant, passive way of seeking God's will. This kind of attitude is not considered appropriate anywhere else in life concerning God's will. Matthew 7:7 exhorts,

> Ask and it will be given to you; seek and you will find;
> knock and the door will be opened to you.

When I wanted to know what college I should go to, I did not just sit back and wait for a college to come and approach me. I prayed, I sought advice, I visited colleges . . . and I found God's will for my life. That has to be part of the attitude we have in dating too. For instance, God did certainly bring Mandy and I together. But I believe that we (our free wills) also played a part in it. The first day I saw her in church I asked her out to lunch. I did this repeatedly for months until she finally said yes. As an act of my will I pursued her, and I believe that was all part of God's plan.

Let me describe another way that people take this too far. People often feel that since God is working behind the scenes to draw you to your spouse, then it is assumed the first person you fall in love with is your spouse. Or maybe, the first person you think is "the one" must be "the one." I understand this feeling. It is a very nice sentiment, to think that we will be drawn to only one person, and that person will be the one we will spend the rest of our lives with. But it is very unrealistic.

God has created us to be drawn to many people. That is where obedience comes in. We need, as in every area of life, to listen to God and be obedient so that we can find God's best for us. It is quite possible to get into a relationship, truly believe you have found the one, and then have God show you that you were . . .. wrong! I know it's hard to believe, but why do we assume that people will not make mistakes in this area of life? It is unrealistic and unfair to put this pressure on young people to say—"The first person I love is 'the one.'" Where is that in the Bible? Why does that have to be our rule? What is good about that? What happens if the first person you love is abusive? Or is simply not right for you? What then?

It seems like it will protect you from sin, however more often than not it creates this pressure-filled atmosphere where people get trapped. And then when they break up, because of this misconception that they must stick with their first choice, they feel lousy about themselves. They have missed "the one." Maybe they will never find "the one!" And that leads to despair, guilt, and shame.

Which brings me to my last point on this. God loves you. He really does. He is not trying to make your life so impossible to figure out that you will inevitably end up unhappy. He promises, in fact, in Jeremiah 29:13-14 that if we seek him he will be found by us! That is great news. Some people enter this process fearing they will never find the one—or at least fearing that they will make a mistake and end up with the wrong person. And the truth is that if you stay humble and submitted to God and people around you—he won't let that happen to you!

Therefore, although God does indeed Sovereignly draw us together, we play a major part. And since he allows us to play a part in the process, we will most likely make some mistakes. This has to be allowed. It is not a sin to be drawn to someone, fall in love, and then figure out you are not meant to be together. That is not a sin. In fact, that is great! I wish more people would figure that out instead of getting married to the wrong person. That is healthy and Godly—it is being obedient to God's will in your life.

Misconception #2
God Would Never Tell You to Date Someone He Knows is Not Your Eventual Spouse
In the last section I talked some of how we will make mistakes in our quest to "find the one." That is very true, and I think breaking up is something that is beneficial and healthy to get us out of those mistakes. But there is a problem with calling them mistakes. When people hear "mistakes" they think you either misheard God, or you stepped out of his will in disobedience. When I say mistake, I am not implying that the person actually did anything wrong. I am simply saying it is a mistake, because it ends up not being the right person in the end.

Let me try to explain what I mean. A committed Christian can start to have feelings for someone and seek God for permission to date them. God can give them permission to date, even though he knows they will not get married. I know that seems radical, but it is true. Look at Abraham for instance. God told him to kill Isaac, even though he knew in the end he would not have to kill him. I know there are some flaws to that analogy, but the principle stands true—God can tell you to do something that he will later change.

We expect this in all other areas of life. For instance, God may call me to go to graduate school but at some point he may tell me to stop. God may call me to go to Africa for a missions trip, but at some point he may call me to come home. Why then, can't God call me to date this one person, and then call me to stop? Why is that so hard to accept? Generally, it is hard for people to accept because overall they view dating as bad. It leads to sin, so why date more than you need to?

What I am trying to show you, though, is that dating can be a God-given tool used to learn more about who "the one" will actually be. Another reason it is hard to accept this way of thinking is Misconception #3:

Misconception #3
You Are Betraying Your Eventual Spouse by Dating
This is ludicrous. Sorry if that is a little too strong, but really—if this is not a scare tactic used by Christians to keep younger Christians from dating, then I do not know what one is. The only way I could betray my spouse before we entered into covenant with each other is if I crossed boundaries physically with someone before marriage. I would be stealing something from her that was intended only to be hers. To say that merely dating robs something from your wife has no basis in scripture or in real life.

Let me tell you why—no matter what you have with other people, no matter how close you get, how committed, how good of friends, even how much you both want to be married . . . in the end it will not compare to what you will have with your spouse. Mandy and I both decided it was a good idea for me to be very open in this book because I want you to know that I am a real person—so here goes: I kissed several girls before dating Mandy. Kissing is definitely something that I consider to be very special and I did not just kiss anybody, but the fact is I kissed several girls who in the end did not end up being my wife. Mandy also kissed some boys before she met me. So, did we rob each other of that gift?

In my opinion, no. Now, I understand that some of you feel a personal conviction to wait until you are married to kiss. This will guarantee that you do not kiss anyone other than your wife or husband. That is very cool, and I honor you in that. But I know there are many out there for whom that simply is not true, and I want you to know that there is something totally different and special about the relationship you have with the person you end up marrying. Nothing can compare to it. I thought I was in love with some of these other girls, and indeed I still think I was, but it comes nowhere near what I have felt for Mandy ever since we started dating. Words cannot describe it—but it is powerful, real, honest . . . different than anything else on earth. I have never once thought that she betrayed me by kissing guys before we were together. I am not teaching here that you should be promiscuous with your kissing either—I outline some careful guidelines to follow in a next chapter on physical holiness. Please read it.

When I express my feelings that these three misconceptions are used as fear tactics to scare young people away from dating in some last ditch effort to keep them virgins, I am not trying to be mean. I see the effects of the faulty thinking behind these theories of dating that are being adhered to in such a widespread fashion in my generation. I am not bashing the Church or Christianity—I am just as much a part of both of those as anyone else! I

want to challenge us and to sharpen us. I just wanted to clarify that—I am
not angry at Christianity per se, I am angry at the effects of this pressure
upon teenage and young adult Christians   .

Lastly, a lot of what I said in this section is most likely hard for
many. I am sure some people will disagree with my take on the three
misconceptions. That is fine. Regardless of whether you agree with my ideas
in this section, the point still stands that the pressure to find and date only
one person, and end up marrying them, has created an atmosphere in which
breaking up is extraordinarily painful. The expectations teens and young
adults feel to perform—to have a relationship that is not a failure—result in
guilt, shame, and despair if a relationship does not end up in marriage.

This simply is not God's heart for his people. He does not want
his children beaten up for trying to follow his will! Most of these people
are honestly seeking God every step of the way—they follow God into the
relationship, and then they follow him out. For anyone to sit in judgment on
them is totally against the spirit of what Jesus has taught us.

We are called to encourage one another, to believe in one another, to
edify one another. Jesus said he came to save and not to condemn (John 3:17).
He is a God of redemption—and he can and will redeem any relationship.
He will bring good out of it, and take you into the next steps of your life.
It is the enemy's plan for your life to drag you down and beat you up with
guilt—to call you a failure for breaking up. It is God's plan to free you
from condemnation, give you hope, and shine his light on your path as you
continue to walk in his will. So that is my heart—let us stop creating an
atmosphere that shames people for breaking up; let us stop labeling a break up
as a failure; and let us begin to be like Jesus in these people's lives. Encourage
them. Help them learn from their past relationships. And lead them to find
God's will in their lives.

Problem #4
Marrying the Wrong Person for the Wrong Reasons
The last symptom of this culture of pressure is one that I have not seen yet.
Truthfully, I hope to never see it, but it is a logical progression from what
I have seen already. Think about the turmoil and struggle of people who
are in a courting relationship, trying to make it the only one they ever have,
and then breaking up and feeling they have failed. It only makes sense that
perhaps some people, because of the pressure and expectations to not break
up, will indeed choose to stay together when God is calling them apart. That
is a great fear of mine when I look at my generation. Some people will end up

going through with marriage, not because God has led them to it, but because it would be too embarrassing, too much of a "failure" based on today's faulty principles of dating, for them to endure. So instead of breaking up with someone who is not right for them, they continue on into marriage simply because of cultural pressure.

I have seen people do many things in life because of external pressure (like peer pressure) and the desire to be liked. What makes this pressure even more powerful is that it is couched in talk of God's will for your life. What Christian doesn't want God's will for their life? So what our culture has unfortunately done has taken peer pressure, and added to it the pressure of potentially letting God down. People now feel that not only have they failed, but also they have somehow let God down, missed his will, or misheard his voice. Do you see the power in that which is greater than mere peer pressure? You are young Christians, people who want to follow God. So to add to the mix a sense of failing God—of course some people will feel it is better to get married than to deal with breaking up.

So this is a possibility. Therefore, we need as the Church, to begin to create a new environment in which my generation can feel free from the bondage of guilt and shame that we put on them and be free to make the right decisions. Christianity should be encouraging people to get out of bad relationships, not pressuring them to stay in them solely for the sake of only courting or dating one person your whole life! In the next chapter we will look at some new ways of viewing dating that will help us do this. Is it possible for dating to be used by God in our lives? I think so. We need a paradigm shift.

Small Group Discussion Questions:

Have you ever felt the pressure to not date until you have found "the one?" If so, where did this pressure come from and how have you responded?

Do you believe that the first person you date should be the person you marry? If so, what do you think of the ideas presented by Christian proposing that it is fine to date more than one person before getting married?

According to this chapter, what are some dangers of believing that the first person you date should be the person you marry?

Do you think God could ever tell you to date someone He knew you would not marry? Why or why not?

If you date someone and then do not end up marrying that person, do you think you have in some way betrayed your eventual spouse?

How would it make you feel if it really was alright to date someone even if you did not know for sure they were "the one?"

Is dating a sin?

A paradigm shift for how we view dating

I have written a lot about the problems with the current belief system of modern Christianity concerning dating. There are philosophical and scriptural problems, as well as problems evident from the negative fruit it is producing. Now I want to shift gears and describe some ideas for looking at dating in a new way.

The Terms

First, I want to define some terms for this book. I have heard people use words like dating, dating-around, courting, friendship, going-out, etc. I view relationships as a continuum from less serious to more serious. The first level, then, would be acquaintance. This is a time in a relationship when you have just met or have only known each other for a short time, and you truly do not know anything deep about each other. A person can also be an acquaintance simply based on the fact that you do not know each other deeply, even if you have "known" them for a long time. During this time, many people fall into infatuation.

I am surprised by how many people start "dating" relationships out of infatuation and not friendship. A typical scenario is a person goes to a Christian concert or conference, meets someone who is attractive and nice, and after hanging out for a couple of days, they are "boyfriend-girlfriend." Often this turns into a long-distance relationship then, and here comes

Instant Messenger! Obviously, that is not the best time to start a committed relationship.

The next level is friendship. Granted there are many levels to friendship. You can have friends whom you know a little, and friends who are as close as family. Friendship differs from the earlier levels based on time spent together and the depth of sharing that has occurred between the two people. At some point let us assume that two "friends" become interested in each other. This means that based on what they see in their friendship, they have found a desire to be around each other and know the other person more and more. This will go through many levels of hanging out a lot, talking on the phone a lot, writing notes, going out to the movies and ice cream until one day a conversation happens and you are dating.

I define dating like this—it is a committed, exclusive, romantic relationship. Committed—this is not just a passing whim, or one night out to dinner; this is a decision on both people's parts to stay together through some difficult times because they are interested in finding out where the relationship will go. Exclusive—both people are committed only to each other, no one else. Romantic—this is not merely a good friendship, but has grown into something where at least the beginning stages of what many people call "love" are starting to be felt. There is affection for each other beyond what you would share with a friend.

The next stage is engagement. Obviously this is when a person asks the other to get married. This is when both people are decidedly strong about marrying each other, and are making preparations. And that clearly leads into the last stage, which is marriage.

Notice that I left out courting. This term is used a lot by people my age, and I have come to understand it as—having a committed, exclusive, romantic relationship with someone who you know you will marry. The major difference between that view and mine is the need to know that you will marry this person. For some these words are largely inter-changeable, however since I do not agree with the whole idea of "knowing whom you will marry" right away, I have chosen to not use this word because it might cause some confusion.

Dating Is Not a Sin

The beginning of the paradigm shift is realizing that dating is not inherently sinful. Nothing in the Bible says that dating is wrong. Dating should not be taken lightly, and we should not commit ourselves to every person we become attracted to. But dating should not be avoided like the plague.

I even, dare I say it, think it is all right to go on "dates" without any underlying understanding of commitment or exclusivity to each other. Assume you are interested in someone and you want to get to know him or her better. What is one way to do this? Talking! Good idea. To talk we need to either use the phone, Instant Message, Email, or actually talk face to face. Assume you want to be as real as possible so you agree to talk in person. It is kind of awkward to call someone and say, "Can we sit down and talk because I want to get to know you" so maybe, just maybe, you go out to dinner together. Now—what is so wrong with that? Nothing! Why is it wrong for two mature Christians to go out on a date just to get to know each other better? There is absolutely no reason. I often encourage my young adult friends to stop analyzing people from a distance and take a chance on a date.

Let me tell you a story . . . Once upon a time I was single. Very single. I prayed for God to bring me a wife almost every night, and yet I never found so much as even a girlfriend for 3 years. Then one day Mandy came to church because her sister had started attending. I can remember the first day she walked in to church (I can actually remember exactly what she was wearing!). That very day, I went up to her and asked her if she wanted to go to lunch after church. Was that too forward? No! I did not think I liked her, or loved her, or wanted to marry her—I just thought it made sense. Here is my logic—"I am single. I feel like God has told me I will be married someday. I am actively on the lookout for this person. A beautiful girl walks into church. She meets all of my immediate requirements (I had known her as a friend since 6th grade so I knew she was a good Christian, etc), so why not? What do I have to lose?" And the answer to that is—nothing. If you go out to lunch, and no sparks fly—great, you are now better friends. But, if you do not ask, you risk losing everything—because you may have missed a chance to get to know this person, and who knows—maybe marry them! Remember my theory—God is (in most cases) not going to reveal your wife or husband to you in a dream or through an angel or by writing it in the clouds—you have to make an effort, and he will lead you.

So I asked Mandy out to lunch, how many times? I lost count. She (for some weird reason) did not get it. Then one day her mom said to her— "Mandy, I think he likes you." She still did not think that was possible. But I pursued. After a night meeting I told her we should discuss gifts of the spirit in the Bible (she had some questions) so I invited her to go get some ice cream, and we went. Our first date (at least I call it our first date—to her we were actually just talking about the Bible!). Wow. And to think I did not know that she was the one. That must have been sin! Sorry I am being a little sarcastic, but it is obvious to me—going on dates, and committed dating are not wrong! Sure, dating can be used to sin, and even to hurt people. But that is true about almost everything, even things that are usually very good. The Bible can be used to sin, and to hurt people (throughout history people have mis-used texts to support all sorts of atrocities) so should we stop reading it?

Back to my main point here—dating is not a sin. It is important to expose the fact that much of the pressure we feel from today's culture is built upon the premise that dating is a sin. We need to rethink why we believe dating is so bad. Is it because dating carries some evil within its nature, or because God has taught us in the Scripture that it is sinful? Or is it because we fear that it could be mis-used so we try to keep people away from it. God can use going on dates and dating itself for good in our lives. I again am not encouraging people to go on dates with every person in the world. There need to be guidelines for purity and accountability, of course. But going on some dates is very healthy and Godly.

I have two provisos though. First, I think there is a difference between teens (especially younger teens) and young adults (please read the introduction for more clarity on this). Younger teens who are still under the direct authority of their parents need to be obedient to their parents, and to follow their guidance. Also, younger teens may not be emotionally or spiritually mature enough to handle getting to know people through going on dates. I think the teen should be open with his/her parents about dating, and together a decision can be made in each individual case. Second, everything I say is tempered by what I write about in my physical holiness chapter—please read it. I never encourage people to go around kissing, or even holding hands with lots of people. I think physical affection is very special and needs to be guarded, so please read that chapter before you judge what I have written here.

A main goal of mine in writing this little section is so young adults can learn to feel free to pursue and get to know people of the opposite sex. Whether you call it dating or not, it is important to be free to hang out one on one without this huge cloud of pressure and judgment hanging over your heads. Christians have overreacted to the secular culture by banning dating all together. However, there is a healthy balance, where one can enjoy dating in a Godly, pure, and holy way. And this dating can then be used as a tool to find God's will in your life.

Dating Is a Tool—Use It To Find "The One"

Once you can separate yourself from the notion, or feeling, that dating is sinful, then you can begin to think about the positive effects it may have on your life. This is the second part of the paradigm shift: seeing dating as a tool that helps you find "the one." Many people my age are sitting on the sidelines. They are maimed by their views of dating, and are unable to enter into relationships deeply enough to find real meaning about the other person. That is where dating comes in. Again there are two levels to this:

First there are dates. This is totally different than committed dating. At some point dates are important, however many people will not want to call them "dates." In fact, Mandy and I did not call our first "date" a date—we were just going out to get ice cream together and talk. A couple weeks later I went to her house to watch a movie with her and two friends. We did not call this a date either. So, what is my point here? It is not so much going on an official "date" that is important, it is the act of being bold enough to go do something alone with that person that matters.

You see, rather than waiting on the sidelines for someone to fall in love with you or for God to write your names on the wall and draw a heart around them, maybe you need to be more proactive. What is wrong with pursuing a relationship with someone? Not a pressure filled relationship with all these unspoken expectations like we have been talking about—but simply a Godly relationship. Just getting to know one another. If you never try to be alone with this person, talk to this person, hang out in normal life situations, how will you get to know them? If you really want to know whether you want to commit to them in a more serious way, how will you know if you do not spend some time together? So my first point here is "going on dates" even if you do not call them "dates" can be a great tool, even a necessary tool, towards discovering more about this person and how the two of you relate.

The second level is dating—committed, exclusive, and romantic. Some people will argue that this first level (which I just described as going on dates) is as far as you need to go. Some would say that you just need to be friends with lots of people, and occasionally its alright to go out with someone one on one, but you should never commit to someone until you are convinced they are the one you want to marry. Granted, some people may know quickly, but the vast majority will not, and that is where a committed dating relationship can be so useful, telling, and powerful. The purpose of dating people is to find a mate, right? So what does marriage look like? Does it look like a relationship where there is no commitment, no romance, no exclusivity, no danger of getting into arguments, and no discussions of "couple issues" like how you treat one another, how you act in public towards one another, jealousy, hurt feelings, etc? I hope not! Marriage is based solely on commitment and exclusivity. Right? It better be! So when you are looking for someone to marry, to spend the rest of your life with, to relate to every day, every night. . . does it make sense to base that solely on a friendship—even a great one?

Some of you may say right back to me—"Yes! Of course! I want the person I marry to be my best friend!" I totally agree. Mandy and I were certainly best friends (and still are!), long before I even thought to ask her to marry me. That is not the point—I am not bashing friendship. Friendship is surely the soil from which a solid relationship will grow. What I am saying is that friendship alone is not a good predictor for how your relationship with that person will look in marriage! By definition it simply cannot be. Friendship does not carry with it all of the weight that a committed dating relationship does.

That is why dating is such a good tool—it is like practice. I have coached a lot of soccer teams, and if someone wants to play goalie, I will not simply throw him into the game, right? I will evaluate him in practice first, and then make a determination. And if he is not good at goalie, I will look for a different position for him. In the same way, rather than jumping into engagement from friendship, it makes sense to spend some serious "practice" time in a dating relationship. This gives you the time you need to analyze and evaluate the relationship to see if you are any good together, and make a wise and Godly determination as to whether marriage will work.

I remember one time during a conference we were holding, a young couple (each 16 years old) came up to me. I had just spoken on some of my ideas about dating. They told me that they respected what I had to say, but they disagreed. They had known each other for something like 4-6 months, and had decided they were meant to be married. So they told their parents, and now they were just courting until they were ready to get married. What? How could they know anything? Did they even truly know each other yet? Did they know what the other wanted out of life? Did their goals match up? Did they know about each other's sin problems? Did they know how the other acted under pressure; when confronted; around the other person's friends; outside of their Christian circle . . .? There are so many questions, and a four month friendship is not long enough to make a judgment for marriage.

Friendship alone will not be able to show you if marriage will work

because people act differently in relationships that involve commitment.
People act differently in romantic relationships. There is so much more
riding on a dating relationship than a friendship—so many more feelings and
so much more vulnerability. And these are areas that must be experienced,
because they are so crucial to marriage. It is easy to be a good friend; it
is hard to be a good (Godly) boyfriend/girlfriend. When I started dating
Mandy, I had so much to learn about love and trust and communication. I
needed almost two years of exclusive commitment to get to the place where
I was ready to get married. If we had stayed friends I would have never
had the opportunity to experience that, to grow, and to become ready for
marriage.

Some people will say that engagement is the time for all that I am
saying. They will say that engagement is the true practice for marriage. I
completely disagree. Sure engagement is preparation for marriage—certainly
the heat is turned up and people's true colors begin to surface even more.
However engagement is not a time to be figuring out whether you are
meant to marry this person or not. And most engagements are actually very
consumed with a lot of distracting things about getting married—planning
the marriage, the reception, the honeymoon, and finding a place to live.
These are all very romantic and exciting things to be doing, but are not real
life. Engagement is a wonderful (though difficult and often stressful) season,
but it is not true to life. That is why I think dating, before engagement,
is such a powerful tool. It mirrors some major aspects of marriage, putting
yourself and your relationship to the test in real life (not in the romantic
whirlwind of engagement), and seeing whether God, you, your partner, and
those around you see this as a relationship that is truly meant to continue
into marriage.

Dating is a great and revealing tool. It can be used to show you both
if you want to get engaged and then married. It is better than friendship
because it has similar elements to marriage, and it is better than jumping
straight into engagement because it is more like real life (which is also where
marriage takes place—real life). This great tool of dating, however, needs to
be used differently than most of us have been taught.

A New Approach To Dating: No More Pressure

I have spent a long time already showing why pressure in a dating
relationship is harmful. When we enter into dating, we should always be
trying to date with the intention of finding a mate. Although I honestly
do not see anything wrong with going on dates for fun, as long as there is

nothing sinful happening, it is wiser to only date people whom you think you could possibly marry (I write in much more detail about this in the "profile" chapter).

While it is important to date with the intention of marriage, it is also important to be balanced about that. Knowing it could happen is different than knowing it will happen. Pressure comes when you as an individual or a couple feel the need to figure out everything right this instant! This is the assumption that must be lifted. You do not need to know. It is all right to date someone and not know whether you will marry or not. My favorite expression is that Mandy and I were "seeing where it would go." That is what dating is. You are both agreeing to commit to getting to know each other deeply, and seeing where it goes. Who knows where it will go—but you will follow God each step of the way, and if you remain submitted, he is faithful to lead you in the right path.

So remove the pressure to figure everything out right away. Be content with getting to know each other—God will show you when it is time to start thinking more seriously about the future. A time will come when you will feel peace to start thinking in that direction (maybe one sooner than the other) and you can cross those bridges when you come to them. But my advice to beginning couples is to steer clear from trying to make those decisions up front. Enjoy relationship. Enjoy getting to know each other better. Enjoy the fun and the learning of dating. And follow God—you can never go wrong when you remain submitted to him and to others around you.

Breaking up is not failure

As we continue to redefine what dating can look like for us, a major issue is breaking up. Breaking up is certainly not painless. No matter how much I tell you that it can be a good thing, that does not mean it will not hurt. But lots of good things in life hurt a whole lot (just ask any woman about labor!). No relationship is without risk. Whenever you allow yourself to become vulnerable, you are opening up the possibility to greater blessing, but also greater pain. Sometimes breaking up is so painful that people avoid going through it, and instead stick with something that truly is not good.

That is why breaking up is so necessary. Breaking up is not failure—it is recognizing that this is not working out how you had hoped, that God is no longer giving you peace to remain in the relationship, and that you simply do not see much of a future with this person. It is an honest assessment that will in the end prevent both people from being more hurt. It is a bold statement and needs to be made to move forward in life. Breaking up is by no means easy, but I believe that God uses it to work in each person's life. Romans 8:28 says,

> In all things God works for the good of those who love him, who have been called according to his purpose.

I see God as a Redeemer by nature. He loves to take things that seem bad, or are bad, and turn them into good. That is why God can turn any break-up into an opportunity. He will redeem you—he will heal you—he will teach you from this experience. Initially breaking up takes some major gusto to go through with because you know people will be hurt—but if you are listening to God, he will make the situation better for both people involved. If you are not obedient you will eventually find God's grace lifting off of your relationship, and even your life. Disobedience is pride, and God says he opposes the proud but gives grace to the humble (1 Peter 5:5). Twice in my life the person I was dating began to go in a different direction than I knew God wanted for me. And even though at the time it was hard emotionally, I knew that I had to follow God first. And he has rewarded me with a blessing I could never have anticipated in those times—Mandy.

I think this redemption carries on in each person's life. After breaking up I believe that God will use that to show you the traits you want in your eventual spouse, and the ones you do not. If we let him, God will teach us from our previous relationships and show us more of what we are looking for in a spouse, as well as traits in ourselves that need refining.

Dating is Not Easy

Briefly, I want to get this out into the open. Dating is certainly very difficult in many ways. Every relationship has risk involved, and dating is no different. Since dating includes a higher level of vulnerability than most relationships, the risk is even greater.

What I am trying to express is this: although I will write a lot about getting rid of pressure at the outset of a relationship, I am not blind to the fact that deciding to actually begin dating someone is a very difficult and involved decision. And that actually bolsters my whole argument here. When you are a Christian who desires wholeheartedly to follow God's will in your life, there are already going to be strong feelings of wanting to make the right decisions. This is natural, and this is one way that being a Christian makes relationships more difficult sometimes. We are very concerned with following God's will, and we never want to make a mistake. That is why it is so wrong to add all this other "outside" pressure to the whole process.

Starting a dating relationship is a hard enough decision already; we should not make it more so. And I want you to know, as you read through this book, that I completely understand the frustration you feel as you are trying to figure out (for example) whether you should share your feelings with someone in your life. These decisions are hard, they are personal, and they are full of emotion. Use this book for guidance in how to best make these decisions in a Godly way.

His Footsteps = Our Pathway
In Psalm 85:13 the author writes,

> Righteousness will go before him, and shall make his
> footsteps our pathway (NKJV).

This verse has been pivotal in my life when it comes to making decisions. I think it carries a very important principle to understand how dating works. When I think about this verse, I picture God taking steps, and leaving behind these enormous footprints. These footprints are so huge that, while they just look like footprints to him, they actually become pathways for me. So I literally want to walk in his footsteps. However, I cannot see all the footsteps at once right? Because God has to take each step one at a time. So this verse teaches me that I cannot know what will be happening thirty years from now—I must be obedient in the moment. I must follow in the footstep that he has provided for me, and not spend lots of time and energy trying to figure out future things that he has yet to reveal to me.

How does this apply to our discussion of a paradigm shift? The old paradigm of dating asks you to try and see all the footsteps up front, all at once. And my paradigm for dating only asks you to see what God is showing you at the time. We need to be obedient in what we can see and enjoy what God has given us now rather than missing what he has given us now by trying to figure out everything in the future. God will reveal his plans for you in his timing. So that means that when you start dating someone and you can not figure out whether God wants you to marry them yet, but you do feel God leading you to date—that you should not worry and fret over it, but simply enjoy the relationship and see where God leads the two of you. Enjoy the discovery process. Enjoy the searching and the seeking of God through relationship.

What Is The Answer For Alan . . . For You?

So I am proposing a paradigm shift in our concept of dating. Rather than seeing dating as this pressure-laden, anxiety provoking, almost evil thing—let us learn to use it to make better decisions about our potential life partners. Rather than allowing fear and intimidation to keep us from dating, let us trust ourselves and each other to be able to create Godly dating relationships. I want to expose and explode the atmosphere of pressure created by Modern Christianity around dating, and give people in my generation a chance to enjoy and grow through dating.

Getting back to Alan, the person I started the first chapter telling you about—this would be my advice to him: First of all, forget trying to figure out whether she is the one right now. Take that pressure off of yourself—most likely you cannot know that now anyway. Does she match up to what you are looking for in a dating relationship? Good. Have you prayed about it? Is God telling you "no?" If not, do you feel peace about moving forward? Then, get to know each other and see where it goes. Have a purposeful relationship—one in which you have decided there is some obvious interest here; let's see what happens as you spend more time together. Do not get too serious too fast. Set guidelines for yourselves, but have fun and enjoy relationship. And allow God to show you in his timing what the next step is (all of this is covered in detail throughout the rest of this book).

I gave a talk last night at a local Christian group of around 100 college age people. I presented my ideas on dating and marriage that are discussed in this book, and the overwhelming response from those who talked to me afterward was that they felt they had been freed. I sincerely hope and pray that this book frees you from the unhealthy pressures that the modern Christian culture can sometimes put on us, and gives you some solid guidance for how to navigate the world of dating and finding a spouse. Rather than running from issues that seem difficult, I want to face them in this book and find what God has to say about them. In him alone will we find the truth, direction, and purpose for our lives that we are ultimately seeking when it comes to dating.

Small Group Questions:
Do you think dating is sinful? Why or why not?

What temptations exist in a dating relationship that you would not encounter if you were not dating?

Do you think that because there are temptations in dating, you should just not date at all, and wait until the day you find "the one?"

Do you agree that dating can be a tool used by God to help you mature and eventually find "the one?" Why or why not?

Why isn't friendship alone a good enough test for whether or not a relationship will work in marriage?

This chapter defines dating as including three main elements that are different from friendship. What are they and why do they make such a big difference?

Is dating a distraction?

Seeking a genuine relationship with Christ

Before getting any deeper into specific issues concerning dating, I must discuss the most important aspect for all areas of life, including dating. A danger with dating and romantic relationships is that they can easily become all-consuming and blind us from what is central in our lives. Our relationship with Jesus must come first. Jesus must be the center, around which everything else in life revolves.

You might find it strange that I spend this much space on having a relationship with Jesus in a book about dating. As you read further, though, you will see that without this relationship with Christ, all of my advice and ideas would be empty because he is truly the source of love, wisdom, and direction. When it comes to dating I believe your love for each other, and the decisions you individually make about your future, must flow from a solid and passionate relationship with Christ.

When I was seventeen, I had been preaching for a couple of years at a bible study we led on Sunday nights. During this time in my life, I was praying virtually every night for my eventual wife. I did not know who she would be, but I knew that I wanted to start praying for her so that God would begin working in her life mightily.

One night while I was praying about her, the Lord spoke very clearly into my heart. He impressed upon me that while I was spending a lot of time praying for my wife, I was not spending any praying for his (the church). He told me to start praying for his wife, and he would teach me lessons about my wife. This pivotal moment in my life set me on a course of pursuing God not just as a Father, not just as the Mighty God, not just as a Savior—but as someone with whom I was falling in love.

Over the past eight years the Lord has taught me repeatedly that this is truly the center of all that will matter in my life—knowing Jesus, loving Jesus, giving myself to him completely. For so long I would use analogies from my dating life to describe my relationship with God, when in reality I needed to be brought back to my first love. If Jesus is truly my first love, then all the other loves in my life will follow after that, be modeled after that, and flow out of that.

This is why I feel it is important to begin a book on dating, romance, and finding a life partner, with a discussion of our love relationship with Jesus. It is my conviction that since God is love (1 John 4:16) then the truest love cannot be shown without Him in our lives—moving through us, changing us, and directing us. The love that I show my wife Mandy must flow from my love with Jesus. I want to love Mandy the way Jesus loves me. And if my relationship with Jesus is where it is supposed to be, then the overflow of that relationship will produce a healthier, stronger, and more intimate relationship with Mandy. That is why I feel this is crucial to address right now, up front. Everything else that we will talk about is lost, if we do not have this.

Falling In Love With Jesus

Not just for dating, but also for life, this will be the most important section that I will write in this book. If you only remember one piece of this book, let it be this. Jesus wants you. He wants to know you. Matthew 7:23 teaches us that Jesus will turn people away in the last days for the mere reason that he does not know them. Christianity is not about religion. It is not about observing certain special days or rules. At the heart and soul of Christianity is Jesus—and having an intimate, real, life-effecting, love-relationship with him.

I want to tell you that there is more to our relationship with Jesus than we know. The scriptures I am about to share with you I use in teachings often. Every time I read them, literally, they challenge me. I am convinced that Jesus has intended a far closer, more personal and intimate relationship between him and his people than many of us ever even pursue, let alone experience.

A very significant, history-altering change occurs in Matthew 27:51

as Jesus dies upon the cross and the curtain to the Holy of Holies is torn in two. Hebrews 10:19-22 explains the significance of this:

> Therefore, brothers, since we have confidence to enter the
> Most Holy Place by the blood of Jesus, by a new a living
> way opened to us through the curtain, that is, his body ... let
> us draw near to God with a sincere heart in full assurance of
> faith...

The temple curtain was torn signifying that all believers were now not only allowed into the Holiest Place (God's true presence) but we were told to pursue him—to "draw near" with "confidence" or, as the NKJV translates it, with "boldness." Why did Jesus die on the cross? "For God so loved the world . . ." (John 3:16). He died because he loved us! Christianity, boiled down to its essence, is a love story. It is the story of a Creator desiring to reconnect with his creation. It is the story of a God so loving that he actually humbled himself, became like his creation, and even allowed his creation to kill him, in order to reach out to us, to you. Sometimes it is easy to forget these truths in the midst of "religion" but the core of Christianity is that Jesus' love is calling us to draw near to him daily.

I want to stay with the idea of the Holy of Holies for one more paragraph and use the temple as an analogy for our lives. The temple consisted of the outer court, the inner court, and the Holy of Holies. In the outer court and inner court there were ritual sacrifices conducted. In the Holy of Holies God's presence was housed. I feel in my life so often (and see if you can relate) that my relationship is limited only to the outer courts. Even the things I do to get close to God—reading my Bible, praying, fasting, worship—even these can become rituals so easily if I forget why I am doing them. When our Christianity becomes these motions that we go through, we move into the outer court—but Jesus is calling us into the Most Holy Place. What is the difference? For me the difference is a true connection with Jesus.

Let me give you an example from my life. My wife and I talk every day, but not every time we talk is it a revelation of the depths of our hearts. I have found that there are several levels to our talks. Sometimes we need to talk about what we will buy at the grocery store—not very deep. Then sometimes we will have good discussions about topics we are thinking about in our lives. These connect us a little more. Then there are times when the connection we have goes beyond the words we are saying to each other. I remember a time when I came into the bedroom and found Mandy crying. It was a difficult time in life for her. Instead of talking immediately and asking what was wrong I just sat with her and held her. After a while of me just being with her something broke loose and she poured out her heart to me. I walked away feeling closer to her than maybe at any time up to that point in our marriage.

The point is this—we can do all sorts of mechanisms (read the Bible, pray, etc) to get us closer to Jesus, but if we never truly connect with the Person of Jesus, then we miss it totally. We need to be with him—we need to spend time with him. We need to get past the outer court and enter the Holy of Holies. We need to get past the forms of worship, and get into Jesus. I know this sounds a little abstract, but bear with me; it will grow more concrete in your heart. There are three examples of this in Scripture that have always challenged me—examples of people who knew what it meant to be close to Jesus.

David: Yearning for God

When I was about 14, my Bible study leader challenged me to start reading the Psalms. He told me to read one a day and see what I learned. I have attempted to, if not keep that exact practice, at least keep the Psalms in front of me on a regular basis ever since. There is one major, over-arching theme that struck me several years ago, and continues to challenge me—David's unquenchable yearning for God despite the adversity of his circumstances. In other words, no matter what happened in his life, David continued to pursue God, rather than blame him; to need him rather than spurn him.

It started for me in Psalm 63:2 (there is not enough room here, but read the whole psalm!)—"My soul thirsts for you, my body longs for you in a dry and weary land where there is no water." The idea of someone's flesh—physical body—actually longing for God is radical. Just as, when separated, people physically feel that emptiness in their stomach—missing someone—David yearned for God's presence when he was not in it.

> As the deer pants for streams of water, so my soul pants for you, O God. My soul thirsts for God, for the living God. *When can I go and meet with God?* (Psalm 42:1-2, emphasis mine)

Can you hear the longing? Can you hear the crying out? There is a reaching for God that David demonstrates throughout the Psalms. So often we expect God to reach to us, and to grab us out of our circumstances. David, in the midst of doubt and confusion, reached out to God and grasped onto him. These Psalms challenge me so much because they stand in contrast to the emotionless religion we see so much of in this world. I see passion in David. I see passion that is not emotionalism and hype, but is grounded in wisdom, an understanding of God's greatness, and an utter need for him. As I read these Psalms I have to ask myself—"Why do you not cry out to God? Why do you get bored of your relationship with God sometimes? Do you have something David didn't?" In Jeremiah it says that during his generation there was no one who raised himself up and called on the name of the Lord. I do not want to be guilty of the same sin.

God is offering a relationship that is passionate, emotional, intelligent, powerful, supernatural, real, and down-to-earth . . . life changing from every direction. And as humans we are tempted to take all that and simplify it. We want a formula we can understand. We want to get our minds around it. But this relationship is much bigger, more real, deeper, and more meaningful than anything else that exists on earth. We cannot capture this. No. In contrast, we must give up trying to get a grasp on it, and we must lose ourselves totally to it.

> One thing I have desired of the Lord, that will I seek: That I may dwell in the house of the Lord all the days of my life, to behold (or gaze upon) the beauty of the Lord, and to inquire in His temple. (Psalm 27:4, NKJV)

David shows us a depth of devotion that we so often miss. He is focused. He wants to know God and his presence and nothing else comes before that. Sound familiar? "But seek first his kingdom and his righteousness, and all these things will be given to you as well" (Matthew 6:33). There is nothing to know, but to know God—and then knowing God leads you to know everything else. In my experience there is a polarization in the Christian world as to how people think we should experience God— emotionally or intellectually. Those who experience God emotionally put down the intellectuals by saying their minds get in the way of truly feeling God's love, power, and presence. Those who experience him intellectually say the others are not grounded in God's word, and are floating about in an amorphous feel-good fest. I think if we polarize either way, we miss a large portion of God's person. I long for the day when we can truly learn to know and love God with our hearts, souls, and minds. It would be limiting God to say we can only experience God in one way. My challenge to you is to open yourself up to experiencing God in a new way that is truly life-consuming, like David did. To put everything else in second place in your life, behind knowing and loving Jesus. "One thing I seek."

Mary: Intimacy with God

There is another aspect of relating to Jesus that the Lord has been showing me through Mary's life. My hope in the last section was to open our eyes to the existence of a deeper and more meaningful, all-encompassing relationship with Jesus. I want to continue to drive that home with this discussion. I was reading about the death of Lazarus one day, and something odd struck me. As a background to this passage, we know that in Luke 10 Jesus commends Mary for taking time out from serving and instead sitting at his feet and listening to his voice. Later, in John 11, Jesus is approaching Mary and Martha's house, several days after Lazarus their brother has died.

The first to meet him is Martha. She greets Jesus and exclaims in verse 21, "Lord if you had been here, my brother would not have died." Look at how Jesus responds to Martha. He tells her that Lazarus will rise again, and then begins to explain to her that he is the resurrection and the life and that whoever believes in him will never die. She ends the discussion by saying that she believes in him. This is a powerful encounter, showing Martha confessing Jesus as the Christ in front of people, and Jesus stating his dominion over death. However, look at what happens when he and Mary meet.

Mary greets him with exactly the same sentence in verse 32—"Lord if you had been here, my brother would not have died." But look at his response to her! "When Jesus saw her weeping . . .He was deeply moved in spirit and troubled." He then asked her to take him to the burial site and "Jesus wept." What a difference! When Martha makes this statement, he ends up giving her a powerful teaching—a theological lesson. When Mary confronts him, however, he is moved very deeply (the Greek word there connotes a very intense and deep feeling) and in fact is moved to weeping. Martha brings out the teacher in Jesus, but Mary brings out the person of Jesus!

My point is this: I believe Mary got a different reaction out of Jesus because her comment, although verbatim to what Martha said, was coming out of a different relationship. I believe there is some scriptural evidence for Mary being consumed with knowing Jesus and intent on looking into his face, while Martha was more concerned with serving him. What can we learn from this? For me this is a powerful example of intimacy. I read this and think—"I wish that I could move Jesus like that!" I long for that intimacy. I long for that closeness. I long to know Jesus in a way that releases his presence in a personal way.

There is so much to say in this section, I could literally type for hours. I hope that everyone reading this understands what I am trying to convey. In Galatians 1:12 Paul writes, "I did not receive it from any man, nor was I taught it; rather, I received it by revelation from Jesus Christ." This is what I am talking about. Each of us is solely responsible to know Jesus in a personal and real way. Paul did not found his Christianity on his doctrines, his teachings, and his knowledge of Scripture—although he was much further advanced in all of that than the majority of his peers. He based his Christianity, in fact his life, in the Person of Jesus. His life and ministry grew out of a personal encounter with Jesus. In fact he also writes that for him "to live is Christ" (Philippians 1:21). Living is being in Jesus. There is nothing else for him. There is no meaning anywhere else, except that which he finds in Jesus. Even his own identity is in Jesus—for he writes in Colossians 3:3 that our lives are "hidden in Christ." So to find who you are, and where you are going—you must search out Christ!

All of this (Mary's example and Paul's writings) proves to me that Jesus intended Christianity to be so much more personal and real than what many of us experience. We have a chance, right now, to be close to Jesus. We cannot wait, we must pursue him now. By pursue him I mean search for him, find him, stay close to him, and become like him. The third person from the Bible that I want to discuss gives us a very practical example of what it means to yearn for God, to pursue that intimacy, and to be close to him.

John: Getting "Close" To God

When I think of someone truly pursuing and knowing how to be intimate with Jesus, I think of the disciple John. John had an incredible closeness with Jesus. He was part of the "three" who were constantly with Jesus. When all the disciples fled from Jesus after He was arrested (Matt 26:56), he and Peter were the only ones to follow. And John, because he knew the High Priest, actually was able to go in "with Jesus" (John 18:15) (he got access for Peter too). Also, when Jesus was dying, he said to his mother, "woman behold your son!"—in reference to John. And John, "from that time on . . . took her into his home" (John 19:27).

Clearly, a special relationship was formed between Jesus and John, and again it makes me jealous. How about you? I see these relationships in Scripture and I begin to long to know Jesus in this way. I wish I could become humble enough, soft-hearted enough, pure enough, devoted enough to know Jesus that way. This is what I am talking about, John had something that I do not have. Now, I am not saying that somehow God loved him more. What I am saying is that God's love is already extended to us, but we can change in order to experience His love, and get closer to Him, in a more real way. We are not earning His love; we are learning how to better experience that which is freely given. For example, if my wife loves me, but I never come home to see her, I will not experience her love, will I? Does that mean she doesn't love me? No! You see, it is my job to draw near to her, so that she can draw near to me (James 4:8) and show me her love by being kind, telling me she loves me, talking to me, going places, having fun, etc!

With that said, let's look at one particular example from John's life. During the Last Supper, Jesus declares that one at the table will betray him. All the disciples get upset and fear that it might be them, so they start to ask Jesus who it is. Jesus does not give an answer though, until one particular disciple asks him—the one who was closest (nearest) to him, literally. John was leaning on Jesus' chest. He was close to Jesus, and so he leaned over and said to Him, "'Lord, who is it?' Jesus answered, 'It is the one to whom I will give this piece of bread when I have dipped it in the dish'" (John 13:26).

This has always been significant to me. Do you think that the closer you are to Jesus the better you are able to hear his voice? Maybe even more able to receive revelation from him for your life? For others? I think so. Verse 24 shows us that Peter, in fact, wanted to know who it was too, but he didn't ask. Why? Because he was not close enough to Jesus to hear him speak. He had to "motion" to John for him to ask. Take that as an analogy of our lives. Do you know people who are closer to Jesus than you, and when you have a question about Jesus, you go ask them what they think? I do. While that is good and actually very wise to do, it also spurs me on to get closer. I want to be the one closest to Jesus, right? I do not want to have to rely on those who are leaning on Jesus' chest —I want to lean!

This piece of Scripture has always challenged me, and made me hungrier for intimacy and closeness with God. I want to be close to Him, near to Him. I want to be able to hear His still small voice. I want to know what His plans are for my life, and receive direction. I want to have access to experiencing His love in deeper and more pure and real ways. I want to know "how wide and long and high and deep is the love of Christ, and to know this love that surpasses knowledge" (Eph 3:19). Think about that!! To know something that surpasses knowledge? How huge is his love? I (we) have so much more to discover! But we will not simply stumble across it— we must pursue it. It must become truly our "first love," our primary passion in life.

Remember Your First Love
Why did I spend so long on this subject in a book about dating and finding a life partner? Everything else that I will cover in this book must flow out of a lifestyle of loving Jesus. You will not be able to resist lust without knowing God's love and forgiveness. You will not be able to make a wise decision about dating someone without God's wisdom. You will not be able to make a life-commitment to someone without knowing God's faithfulness, his perseverance, and his will for your life. And even after marriage, you will need so much of who God is in order to be the husband or wife you aspire to become.

I love how Jesus' teachings are poignant across time and culture, for example, the parable of the builder speaks right now, today. If we do not build our lives, every aspect, on the rock of Jesus, we will fall. True blessing, success, joy, happiness, peace, security, love, and direction all exist in Jesus alone. If we desire for our lives to be blessed, for our relationships to be full of life, and for our marriages to be wonderful we need to be based, rooted, and founded upon a faith and love relationship with Jesus.

I hope it is clear that it would be against my conscience as a writer, a Christian, and a friend to start this book with anything else. To simply give you loads of advice, but not give you the soil to plant it in would be equivalent to teaching you how to sky dive but never giving you the parachute. If you are not a Christian I challenge you to investigate Christianity. Read the Bible and judge for yourself; don't rely solely on what others say about the Bible. If you are already a Christian, I challenge you to put your faith to the test. In so many of our lives, there is more for us with Jesus. There is a relationship waiting to be had behind that religion. There is a deep, heart connection, a meaningful knowing that goes beyond words. Search for God and find him—over and over again. I want to live a lifestyle of pursuing Jesus and finding him and his love and power repeatedly throughout my life. I challenge you to do the same, to never become complacent.

I want to end this chapter with some verses I read to Mandy the day I asked her to marry me. I chose these verses on purpose because this book (Song of Solomon) had first come alive to me in my relationship with

Jesus. This book has taught me volumes about the intimacy that God desires with us, the love he has stored up for us, and the pursuit of our relationship, both me after him, and him after me. But as I fell in love with Mandy I also understood these verses in relation to her. As I set the Lord as a seal upon my heart, now I was asking Mandy to do the same. To know that I was going to choose to love her forever, that my love for her would never die, and that the "many waters" of this world could not drown it out. All of this can only be true though, when that love is flowing from my intimacy with Jesus.

These verses are very poetic, and some of you may wonder what they really are saying. They certainly do need to be interpreted. I am by no means a master poet, but I will tell you what they mean to me. It begins by stating that love is something inward (heart) and something outward (arm) that others can see by my actions. It shows that love is a choice (set me as a seal) and a passion (vehement fire) in one—and that this passion is so much more powerful than the powers of this world (even death!). It also argues that true love cannot be tamed or discouraged by the world or circumstance. Finally it says that you cannot buy love (don't start singing the song now); it is a free gift. And because it is a free gift it cannot be used in wrong ways (manipulation) but must freely be given, or it will be despised. So there is my stab at poetic interpretation. It teaches me a lot; maybe you will find more meaningful insights for your life. In any case, here it is:

Song of Solomon 8:6-7 (NKJV)

Set me as a seal upon your heart,
As a seal upon your arm;
For love is as strong as death,
Jealousy as cruel as the grave;
Its flames are flames of fire,
A most vehement fire.

Many waters cannot quench love,
Nor can the floods drown it.
If a man would give for love
All the wealth of his house,
It would be utterly despised.

Small Group Discussion Questions:
According to Christian how does your relationship with Jesus impact your current or future dating relationships? Do you agree?

Of the three people used as examples – David, Mary, and John – whom do you feel most accurately describes your relationship with Jesus?

Which of the three – yearning, intimacy, and closeness – is hardest for you to foster in your relationship with Jesus and why?

Do you think it's true that the closer you are to Jesus the easier it is to hear His voice?

Why is it important to continually pursue and renew our relationship with God?

What do you think are the dangers of "letting up" in our pursuit of God?

In your own words, what does it mean to be "close to Jesus?"

Are you satisfied with where you are in you relationship with Jesus? Why or why not?

What is something you could work on to create a more genuine and deep relationship?

Is it alright for Christians to date non-Christians?

How to know what you're looking for, before you find it

Some of the best decisions I made regarding my relationship with Mandy came before I ever was even interested in her. Sometimes people feel that when they do not have anyone in their life that is a "possibility," there is nothing effective they can be doing for their eventual spouse and/or eventual marriage. There are plenty of important steps that can be taken during this time. This time can be either highly fruitful or it can be wasted, and it all depends on our outlook.

I am writing this assuming that you are interested in getting married someday. Please do not misinterpret what I am saying here to mean that marriage is the end all and be all, and that every single person should be pining for marriage because there alone lies true fulfillment. That is something that single people feel sometimes, but it is a horrible misrepresentation of the truth. All we have to do is look at Paul's discussion in 1 Corinthians 7 concerning how unmarried men and women can serve the Lord unhindered because they are not married. Therefore we can see that being single is no way inferior to being married. So please do not think that I am saying that.

What I am saying is that many single people hope to be married someday—and there are two attitudes single people can have. Some people go through this "waiting" time feeling horrible and discontent; others go through it, still feeling a lack, but taking advantage of the time. Ephesians 5:16 tell us to make "the most of every opportunity, because the days are evil." This is such an important principle for any time in life, and it applies powerfully to the single time in life as well. What can we do to make the most of the time before we find the person we want to marry? Approach this time with a new attitude—a redeeming attitude—one that will not allow this time to go to waste.

The Profile

When I was growing up, my Dad and I used to take a ski trip in the winter every year. This was great fun for many reasons, but one of the best was the three-hour trip both ways. My family has always been incredibly busy, so we all have needed to make time to talk—this was one way my Dad and I did this. After a couple years, this trip became a kind of "annual check up" on some major issues in my life.

One question my Dad always asked on these trips was, "So, have you thought any more about what you are looking for in a wife?" This is a great question. And my answer would end up being this checklist that would get refined every year based on lessons I had learned through God, personal growth, and dating. For instance, when I was 16 I dated this one girl. The best part of our relationship was how much fun we had together. We were friends before we dated, and the reason we ended up dating is because we could be crazy and fun around each other. The relationship did not work out for other reasons, but I walked away knowing something I honestly did not know: I wanted someone with whom I could have fun. I wanted someone who was not dreary and serious, and who could be crazy and occasionally impulsive. So that year, when we took our ski trip, we talked about that, and I added it to my list. Three years later, when Mandy and I started hanging out and becoming better friends, I quickly realized that she had a perfect balance of being able to have serious, intense talks—and being able to be crazy and do stupid stuff and have fun.

What emerged in my life, largely due to these conversations, is what I now call a "profile." A profile is a list of qualities, characteristics, and traits that you are looking for in a spouse. This profile will benefit you in a couple ways. First, it crystallizes your thinking process about who you are looking for. Many people do not even think about this; they just go through life and whoever they are attracted to becomes the person they end up being interested in. This profile forces you to think about the decisions you make, and therefore brings clarity to your search. Second, the profile can act as a buffer—a first line of defense—against starting to date the wrong person. Imagine you are at youth conference. You meet this really great guy. He is cute and seems like a good Christian. You are very excited and give him your email address. Then, a couple days later over Instant Messenger, he asks you if you believe in the gift of tongues. You reply, "no"—because you are a cessationist. He begins to talk about how he can't imagine being a Christian and not speaking in tongues. So what happens next? Many people would let that slide and continue on in relationship. Eventually they might fall in love because they like a lot of things about each other, but then at some point they realize that their doctrines are so different that they would never even be able to attend the same church . . . and they must break up.

If you had created a profile that required your boyfriend to have similar doctrine, you could avoid that story completely. This is not to say this would never work (I have two friends for whom it did work because they came into unity over time) but making a profile protects you from giving your heart out in situations that are doomed from the beginning. When I was single, I could usually surmise if someone fit my profile within a few hours of talking to someone new. Sometimes less!

You can be attracted to anyone. You can fall for anyone who makes you feel special, meets your needs, and touches your heart. But God does not just want "anyone" for you—he wants the best. The profile acts as a filter to help you begin this process of discerning the bad, the good, and the best. Now, you can't determine for sure if someone is the "best" until you have spent much time in a relationship, but the profile makes your chances a lot better than simply making the decision based on attraction. If a girl made it through my profile, I was excited to get to know her because maybe this was it!

In a profile there are generally two lists. First is the list of "definites," or traits you must have. Second is the list of personal traits you have come to know that you want but may not necessarily need.

"Definite's"—"Do Not Be Yoked Together Unequally"
There is absolutely no "gray area" when it comes to Christians wanting to date non-Christians. Many people try to rationalize this, or get around it, even though 2 Corinthians 6:14 (NKJV) explicitly states:

Do not be unequally yoked together with unbelievers.

I have heard over my teenage years a vast array of arguments trying to push this truth aside. The crux of all of these arguments is that "yoked" is only referring to marriage and not to dating. However, there is no reference at all to marriage *or* dating in these verses. This section of Scripture ends with this: Paul states, "therefore . . . let us cleanse ourselves . . . perfecting holiness in the fear of God" (7:1, NKJV). Paul is talking about holiness here. So the "unequally yoked" principle has nothing to do explicitly with marriage; it has to do with any kind of yoking that would then lead us to unholiness.

The question then becomes, what is yoking? The imagery of yoking refers to a wooden bar shaped to fit around the necks of two oxen, and connected by a pole to something they are pulling. When Paul uses the word "yoking" he is referring to two people joining their lives together, becoming united in a close and intimate way. Paul is not stating here that we should stay away from relating to and being friends with people who are not Christians. That would be antithetical to Jesus' teaching and the rest of the New Testament. However, dating is not simply a relationship with an non-Christian. Dating is joining your lives together in an intimate way. You are deciding, for a time, to put both of your lives on the same course, and to be joined in your lives until you either get married or break up. This is yoking beyond a doubt. And Paul is very forthright in denouncing it.

However, let us assume Paul does not denounce it. Does it even make sense for a Christian and a non-Christian to date? I am finding more and more as I get older that the truth in the Scripture just plain makes sense. So when Paul tells us something like this, there must be a reasonable explanation. It is simple—if you are a Christian, what matters most to you in life? Jesus does! Paul wrote in Philippians 1:21 that for him, "to live is Christ." This should be true of all Christians. Jesus said that to follow him meant to give up everything else and pursue him alone (Luke 9:23). Paul also said in Philippians 3:8-10 that he counted everything he had attained in this world—heritage, social standing, prestige, prominence, good works—loss for the simple fact that he wanted to truly know Christ. And lastly, in Matthew 22:37, Jesus tells us the greatest commandment of all for Christians is to love God with everything that you are. So to be a Christian—which means to be a follower of Christ—requires that everything else in life becomes secondary, and that Christ becomes the center.

If being a Christian means this all-encompassing and all-consuming devotion to Christ; if it means possessing a faith that determines each step of a person's life—how you act, think, talk, make decisions, and have relationships—then how can a Christian ever truly have a romantic and intimate relationship with a non-Christian? Dating requires sharing our hearts—our deepest thoughts, feelings, fears, and dreams. How can you possibly become truly unified with someone with whom you can never share the most meaningful person (Jesus) in your life? It just does not make sense. And this is not meant to be mean, or to belittle people who are not Christians. I believe we are called to be friends with and to love non-Christians. Jesus spent most of his time with people who weren't "religious." All I am saying is that this simply does not make sense—for the Christian *or* the non-Christian. What person who does not believe in Christ wants to marry someone who would be actively Christian?

With all that said, I hope you will agree that not only does God forbid it—but it is a good idea to not date people who do not believe in Jesus. It just does not make sense. And if you are already in a relationship like that, I know it will be difficult, but get out! It will be better for both of you!

Let's take "do not be unequally yoked" a step further. Should a veteran Christian date a brand new Christian? Should you date someone who has radically different doctrinal beliefs than you? Should you date someone with whom there is a major disagreement from the beginning about something you are passionate about?

Let me tell you two stories. When I was 15 I started to be attracted to this girl—let's call her Lisa. I saw her in church one day and thought—"wow she is gorgeous, I must meet her!" So I met her, and found out that she was not a Christian. So I self-righteously asserted my conviction that I described above, and did not allow myself, even though I liked this girl, to begin any sort of relationship. Even after several months of friendship, when she approached me saying she would be interested in dating, I still did not proceed because I refused to be unequally yoked (I am so holy!). Then one night, on New Year's Eve—I was talking with Lisa about God and faith. And lo and behold she decided she wanted to become a Christian. So we prayed, and I ran outside to my friends who were playing basketball and jumped around and told them—we were all very excited.

So guess what happened next. That's right . . . it took me a whole two hours to decide that, well, she was indeed a Christian, and I liked her . . . so I guess I better date her! My, how great is the goodness of God! He answered me in my time of need by bringing her into salvation (don't mind my sarcasm). I do not doubt her conversion, but what I definitely doubt is my very erroneous thought process that led me to believe that simply because she now had her name written in the book of life, she and I would be "equally yoked." I had been a Christian for 10 years, and she had been one for maybe 10 minutes. What was I thinking? (In the end we broke up because our convictions on very important issues were vastly different, largely because as a new Christian she was still trying to find out what she believed.)

Let me tell you the second story. I have a friend who started to like this guy a whole lot. They are both very mature Christians, and young adults. However they disagreed on one major topic—the role of women in the church. My friend, a girl, believes women have equal ability as men to minister in the church. Her boyfriend, however, felt that women were to remain submissive and quiet. This was disaster waiting to happen. There is no way, if their convictions stayed the same, that they could have continued into marriage. Can you imagine? How could they go to the same church? What would he think when she told him she was teaching on Sunday morning—"Want to come listen, honey?" "No I think you are a heretic!" "OK—pass me the OJ please." I mean how could they have gotten around this? And then think about the home—do you think she is going to want to be "submissive" in the way he would want her to be? No way! If she believes women and men were created equal—she is going to feel that her input on decisions is equal to his; her authority in the house is the same; her ability with finances, children, etc.

Do you see my point from these two stories? Be careful about your yoking. There is no time for yoking around (ha!). Dating is a mechanism to help you find your spouse. From the beginning you need to rule some people out. So no matter how attractive they are, or how funny, or cute, or whatever—keep your eyes on the prize. This is what a profile will help you do. You will not get distracted, you will keep focused on who you are looking for, and you will not waste time with someone whom you know would never work out in the end anyway.

My list of definites consisted of the following: must be a Christian; must believe the basic same doctrine as I did, especially concerning gifts of the spirit; must attend my church; must attend the youth church that I pastor; and must be very beautiful. I had several other traits that were important to me, but were not absolutes, and these are ones I am calling "Personal Traits."

"Personal Traits"
Physical Attractiveness is an interesting topic to hear some people talk about.

I have heard people say that physical attractiveness is not that important, and what really matters is what is on the inside. I remember I was in a conversation one time with a close friend of mine, and he had just watched some videos about purity in relationships. He told me that after watching the videos he had decided that the most important thing he was looking for in a girl was what was on the inside, and that he would not mind if he ended up marrying someone whom he was not totally and completely attracted to. This made me so sad for him!

Hear me out—a main theme of this book is responding to currents of opinion in the popular Christian culture that I have found to be unhealthy, unwise, and/or unbiblical. This is one of those currents. There is actually a strong "pressure" in the culture to not place too much weight on physical attractiveness. In fact sometimes it goes so far as to imply that to be physically attracted to someone is in some way less Godly or holy! Where does this come from? I think I might know. There are many people who find a lot of meaning in Proverbs 31:10-31. This is a wonderful description of many traits that are great to find in a wife, and none of them mention physical attractiveness—in fact it ends with this:

> Charm is deceptive, and beauty is fleeting; but a woman who
> fears the Lord is to be praised.

I would be a fool to argue with scripture. I agree with it and understand that physical attractiveness will fade, and that it is not the most important trait to look for in someone. However, I feel that some people take this to the total extreme and claim that the Bible teaches that physical attractiveness and outward beauty are worthless, when in fact it does not say that. Of course fearing God, being a Christian, having Christ-like character are most important, but is it right to simply throw out physical attractiveness all together?

Who made our bodies? God did. And when he finished he said that he thought they were good. God purposely made us with bodies, and in fact, when he returns we will be given new bodies. I think that to ignore the importance of physical attraction in finding a mate is to ignore a huge piece of God's gift to humankind. He wants us to enjoy the work of his hands. Have you ever read Song of Solomon? In Chapter 4, starting in verse 1, Solomon begins to talk about the beauty of the one he loves—"How beautiful you are, my darling! Oh, how beautiful! " And he proceeds to describe how much he loves every little physical trait about her—her eyes, hair, mouth, lips, and so on. Is this really in the Bible? Of course it is. It makes so much sense to me—this is how God wants it to be for us. For some reason the church has tried to make people feel guilty about being attracted to the one you love—but that is God's will, it is his gift! Listen to the passion in Solomon's words:

> You have ravished my heart, my sister, my spouse; you have
> ravished my heart with one look from your eyes, with one
> link of your necklace (Song of Solomon 4:9, NKJV).

He does not say—"you have ravished my heart with your Godliness" does he? Please hear me—I am trying to make a point. I am not saying that physical attractiveness is more important than character and relationship with Jesus. But I am saying that it is important and we do not have to feel bad about saying that. I am not ashamed to say that I did not date many people in my life, simply because I knew I was not totally and completely attracted to them. They had great character and loved Jesus—but they did not have that beauty I knew I wanted. But I can remember exactly what Mandy was wearing when she walked into my church the very first day. And I used to go to high school with her before that, and get this—my friend used to tease me because he would catch me looking at her during class. I thought for years before we ever found each other that she was the most beautiful girl in my school. And I can say that when I looked at her, and now when I look at her—that she "ravished my heart!"

Think about it this way—for the rest of your life, you have to look at this person's face every morning when you wake up. So do not feel guilty about placing some importance on this area. I think it is crucial and vital. You do not have to settle for someone who is just attractive to you on the inside—you will find someone who is fully attractive to you, inside and out. And that is an amazing aspect of God's creation—we are all so different from each other. That is what makes "beauty" so relative. Beauty is not what we see on the cover of magazines when we are waiting in line at the grocery store. Beauty is subjective. It is personal. Beauty to one person is not beauty to another. And I think God did this so that everyone will find someone with whom a common attraction is shared, both inside and out, so that they both will be astounded and "ravished" in the heart by each other.

Physical attractiveness is the only "personal trait" that I have a lot I want to say about. Some other traits that may fall under this (just to give you something to start you thinking) are: humor, creativity, spontaneity, ability to think deeply, ability to talk seriously, share the same likes and dislikes, have life goals that fit with yours etc. This is certainly not an exhaustive list. It is meant to start you thinking. I encourage you to sit down and think this through, talk to people, talk to your parents, talk to people you respect—and come up with a profile. It creates a starting point to define who you are looking for.

You Will End Up With a Real Person—Not a Wish List

Now that I have said all that, I have to bring some balance. While I believe that it is important to make a profile and to know what you are looking for in a mate, it is vital to understand that you will not marry that list—you will marry a person. And by definition, people are imperfect. Many people (even if you do not have a profile) have an ideal in their mind about whom they want, and often this ideal becomes completely unrealistic. You create a person in your mind who simply cannot exist.

In the end love is a choice, and we will talk about this more in other chapters. But love, ultimately, is not a feeling and goose-bumps—it is a choice. I chose to love Mandy for the rest of my life no matter what happens. And part of that choice is choosing to love the person despite their faults. Every person is going to have shortcomings. This is important to understand because many people enter into dating relationships (and even marriage) expecting this person to measure up to this perfect ideal. Then when real life sets in they realize that is not true, and become disillusioned and frustrated.

There is an important balance here however, because I am not saying that you should settle for someone who simply is not right for you. Mandy made the choice to love me, even though I occasionally have an anger problem. This is one of my weaknesses that she came to know during our dating, and had to make a conscious decision to say, "Yes, I know he has an anger problem, but I want to choose to love him in spite of, and through that." Now, the story would be different if I had a physical abuse problem. If she were to find that out in our dating, she certainly should not decide to "love me in spite of that." That would be plain foolishness. I know that is an extreme example to make a point, but you need to know what you are willing to love someone through, and what is definitely not going to work for you—and that is the whole idea behind the profile. It is just like a map is something that points you in the right direction, but is not the actual road itself. When you get on the actual road there may be some potholes not shown on the map, but it still takes you where the map said it would. In the same way the profile is the map, it will point you in the right direction, but you can not expect the actual person to be exactly like the profile.

There is also another way in which the profile must be flexible. Not only will this person be a human and therefore imperfect and not an ideal—God may also choose to alter your profile slightly for your best interest. For instance, Mandy has almost everything on my list that I wanted. But there are some traits that I wanted, that were not truly what I needed. An example is this: I thought that the person I married was going to be someone with similar gifts as myself. Therefore I expected that she would be speaking in front of lots of people and leading worship. And for a couple of years, I tried to force Mandy into that role. It turns out that she has very different gifts than I do and that God intended it that way. She has many gifts, but when I think of her the first thing that comes to mind is sacrificial service—laying down her life for others in practical ways through prayer, counsel, financial support, and gifts. These character traits didn't come as easily for me, but they are so crucial! God put us together perfectly, and we balance each other out wonderfully.

Therefore, even though I was surprised by some of the traits that my wife has, in the end Mandy is perfect for me. What she offers me through our relationship is more than I could have ever hoped for. However, first I had to realize God had changed my profile a little, and that it was a good thing. When I look back on some of the traits I thought I wanted, and compare them to what Mandy has, I realize that God knew what I needed even more than I did, and he provided for me. I do not think I can express in words the incredible support Mandy is to me. I tend to be an outwardly strong person, but God gifted Mandy to see right through me, keep me honest, and handle my weakness and insecurity like no one else can.

Purity of Thought

While creating a profile is important, there are several smaller points about the time you spend together before dating that are worth discussing. They are important to prepare the way for the will of God in your life in this area. In practicing these ideas you will be creating a solid foundation upon which a healthy relationship will be able to be built.

There is a chapter in this book about physical holiness inside of a dating relationship. However, holiness should not begin only when you are in a serious relationship, but is a cultivated lifestyle regardless of your position in life. During this phase of life (before a relationship) it is easy to begin assessing every person of the opposite sex that we meet by asking ourselves, "Is this person a possibility?" This is good, but there is a danger.

The danger comes when we begin to objectify people of the opposite sex and fall into simply looking at their exteriors and judging them based on that. For many, that sole focus on the exterior quickly slips into the "lust of the eyes" mentioned in 1 John 2:16 (NKJV). My basic caution in this area is this: be extra careful to remain pure in your thoughts towards people of the opposite sex. This purity before a relationship begins will form a strong foundation upon which to build a pure relationship when the time is right.

Personal Growth The Main Goal—Not Finding Someone

During this time before dating it is very important to stay focused on getting closer to Jesus and becoming conformed to His image. For many it is easy to be consumed by thoughts and desires to find a partner, when in reality we should be taking advantage of this time by growing and maturing in Christ. As I said before, the Bible tells us to redeem the time, and to make the most of every opportunity (Ephesians 5:16, NKJV). This means that we should not allow this time to waste away while we wait. We should use this time to grow and become who we are supposed to be in Christ.

I remember this one summer in my life where most of my friends were either engaged or had girlfriends. I was a little upset that I did not have anyone special in my life at the time, but I distinctly felt the Lord lead me into a season set apart for me to grow in evangelism. So, when the weekend would come and I would have no one to hang out with, guess what I did? Evangelism. I would drive to Main Street by myself and walk around and find people with whom to share Jesus. This time in my life, I can see now, was crucial to the development of much of who I am now as a person and as a minister. At all times we need to be seeking to grow in the Lord, whether outside of relationship or inside of one. You never know, God may have something incredible for you right now, that you will not be able to do once you find someone.

Make Lots of Friends

I have a theory that I want to tell you about. The theory is to be friends with as many people as possible when you are single. If I were single right now, I would be hanging out with all sorts of people, guys and girls, in groups and alone—just getting to know people. I have heard some people argue that a guy and a girl should never be alone until they are committed to each other . . .. why not? I ask that question because I do not understand the reasoning. Are people afraid that if you go out for ice cream with a friend of the opposite sex alone, you may end up slipping into sexual sin? I just do not see the connection! Why does it have to be that way?

When I was single, I used to go out with many friends who were girls. I wanted to get to know them more. I wanted to spend time with them. So we would go out for ice cream or hot chocolate (apparently anything that included sweets!) and talk. This was great for many reasons, but here are a couple—1) It gives you a chance to learn how to relate to the opposite sex better. 2) The better you get to know these people, the more you can learn about whether you think that individual is someone you might possibly be interested in. 3) Relationship is a good gift from God—we are meant to enjoy it and have fun!

I am not saying that you should go out with a different person every weekend and end up kissing them or anything—I am not talking about that kind of "dating." I am talking about just being friends with lots of people. The way I think about it is very practical and may offend you, but just give me a chance: if you want to find a church, but you never take the time to go to churches and check them out and spend time there and get to know the people—how will you ever know which one you should go to? In the same way, how are you going to find someone, if you are not out there getting to know people? There is nothing wrong with making friendships; as long as you remain pure in your thoughts and actions and motives, the Lord will bless those friendships and you both will grow.

As I mentioned earlier, the first time Mandy and I went somewhere alone was after a church meeting. I said that I would like to go get some ice cream and discuss spiritual gifts (she had asked me about them earlier)—so we went to Denny's. I now call this our first date. But there was no romantic intention at all that night, we were just being friends and getting to know each other. But we gave God opportunity to work, and I went home, even after that first night, and I thought to myself—"wow, I can't wait to do that again!" Now I get to take her to ice cream any time I want—because she's my best friend. That is where this whole thing has to start—friendship! So why seclude yourself and wait for God to drop a wife or a husband into your mailbox? Go make some friends.

Pray For Your Spouse

This is huge. I do not know where I learned this, but this was such an important part of my growth before Mandy and I began hanging out. I believe it did a lot spiritually to bring us both into places of maturity. For a couple of years I prayed almost every night for my spouse before I fell asleep. I simply made it a habit. I prayed that God would be with her wherever she was, that he would be protecting her, that he would help her to grow in her relationship with him and in her gifts for ministry. This was so cool because I truly felt that I was doing something in the spirit for her already. And it also was setting a great precedent for my eventual marriage. I was serving her. I was praying for her. I was encouraging her to grow in Christ. All of these are foundational aspects of my relationship with Mandy now, and they were birthed in that time of prayer.

Something else noteworthy is that many times when I was praying I felt God give me specific topics about my wife that I should pray about. I now can look back and see that very similar things were happening in Mandy's life at about the same time. Neat, huh? I strongly encourage you to develop this in your life. And this is not prayer simply to just find a spouse soon; it is prayer for your eventual spouse—focused on that person's life and needs. It is truly powerful.

Enjoy Being Single

During this season of your life, you can choose to dive in fully and get everything out of it that you possibly can, or you can decide to wallow in loneliness and misery. It is very tempting to spend a lot of time feeling sorry for ourselves and wishing our lives were different, when what we should be doing is fully enjoying what God has given us.

1 Corinthians 7 can be slightly confusing at times but there is one truth which he makes clear in verses 31-34. Married people need to focus on pleasing their spouses and pleasing the Lord, while single people can focus solely on pleasing the Lord. This is very true—while you are single you simply have more time to do whatever you want. You can use that time to serve the Lord. You can use that time to have fun and to grow.

I have a friend who recently decided to go to Haiti for a month and do some missionary work. I would have loved to have gone with him, but I could not. Another one of my friends recently packed up and went to Australia for four months, just to do something different with his life. I certainly could not do that! If I were single right now, a lot of my life would be different—I would have a lot more time to do things like traveling and spontaneous adventures (like driving across the country). With that said, I do not regret being married. I love having a family, and the responsibilities that come with it. The point is, when you are single you do not have those responsibilities yet—so enjoy your freedom! Take advantage of it!

One main reason that I am happy being married is because I was happy being single. Sure I prayed every night for my wife, but ask any of my friends—I lived life to the fullest. I was going full force in ministry and trying new adventures, I was often out with friends until very late at night. I enjoyed being single. I knew that one day things would change, so I made a conscious decision to live life. I lived in an apartment with four close friends, and often decided to be a little irresponsible and stay up until 4am playing TecmoBowl (a football video game—the best ever). Those were awesome times, and I am so glad for them—now I am not able to see those friends as often, and I certainly cannot play video games with them until 4am. Do you see what I am saying? I enjoyed my single years, and as a result now that I am married, I have no regrets. If you live your single years depressed about not being married—chances are you will end up in your married years, depressed about not being single. Have you ever met people like that? I have—it is so sad! Every stage of life is a gift from God—use it! Enjoy it!

Wisdom To Say No And Courage To Say Yes

Balance is needed when discussing dating. Some people feel afraid to say "yes" to potentially good relationships, and some fail to make wise decisions to say "no" to relationships with no potential. The profile is a powerful tool to help you make these decisions with more objectivity and wisdom.

I want to emphasize the power and importance of saying "no" to people with whom you should not enter into a committed relationship. I have given several ideas for spending the season of your life where you are waiting to find someone in a productive and healthy manner. Having wisdom and self-control in this time is vital. Avoiding the wrong relationships prepares the way for the right relationships to enter your life.

I remember specifically two people I knew when I was 16-19 years old with whom I could have begun relationships. I was very good friends with both of them. They were both great Christians, lots of fun, and we got along very well. However, I knew that I needed to take these decisions seriously so I weighed them before God and allowed Him to direct my heart. In both cases it took a while to know, so I was obedient and waited—insisting we continue simply being friends. And then eventually the Lord showed me (once in the midst of me thinking I liked this girl a lot) that this was not a path He wanted me traveling. So we did not date.

These were both great decisions. And they paved the way for growth in my life, and eventually for meeting Mandy. Therefore, it is important to know when to say "no." However, I am not saying that you should say no every time until something magical and spiritual happens and God reveals from heaven that you have found your spouse. There was one relationship in my life that I did pursue during those years, that I felt totally at peace and released by God to pursue. This person was incredible and a woman of God. We were great friends and everything seemed wonderful. We both learned a lot about life together and about what we wanted in our spouses later in life. . but in the end, we were not meant to be together.

So there is the balance—we must know when to say "no" and be wise and willing to say it. But we must also know when it is good and not wrong to say "yes" even if it does not end up in marriage. The relationship I mentioned above, I would never throw away. In fact, we are great friends still. The rule of thumb I used in order to keep this whole thing in check was this: I was not allowed to date anyone unless I felt they could end up being my wife. Not that they would definitely be my wife—just that they could. This again is where the profile comes in. The profile helps you determine who could fit into the category of "potential spouse," and who should be excluded. This takes self-control on one hand—to say no to people to whom you might be greatly attracted. But it also takes freedom and courage on the other hand—to allow yourself to say yes to people with whom you could see yourself, but will not be totally sure about unless you take the time in a committed relationship like dating to get to know each other. And that is the point of this book. I will say that a lot during the book, so you will know it when you are done!

Small Group Discussion Questions:
Do you agree or disagree with the assertion that Christians and non-Christians should not date each other? Why or why not?

The main point of this chapter is that the time spent before you start dating does not have to be unproductive time. What are things you can do during this time to refine your character and prepare you for dating?

Do you ever pray for your eventual spouse? Why or why not? If you started to pray for him/her, what could you pray?

A "profile" outlines two kinds of "traits" that you are looking for in a potential spouse. Take some time now to make your own profile:

> 1) List those traits that are "definites". This list should include only those things that are non-negotiable for you.

> 2) Next, list those traits (called "personal traits" in this chapter) that you would prefer, but could be flexible on.

How fast is too fast?

Starting a dating relationship

There was a time in my life when several of my friends were all coming to my wife and me for advice about potential romantic interests. After listening to much of the frustration and uncertainty in their stories, I realized that they felt a lack of guidance and direction for how to go about beginning a relationship. Once we remove the stigma of "dating" and become open to exploring the possibility of moving into a relationship with someone we are interested in, how do we do it?

Sometimes I feel that the modern Christian culture has spent so much time railing against dating in general, it has neglected to provide adequate pastoral guidance to those who are maturely interested in committing to a romantic relationship. Relationships are complicated and unique. There can be no textbook for them, and rightly so: one of the most exciting aspects of relationships is the exploration and discovery of how each particular one works. However, having come through the process of dating, engagement, and marriage recently, I hope to be able to provide some general guidelines. In reading the Bible, I find numerous biblical principles that can be gleaned and applied to beginning a dating relationship.

Friendship Dating
"This is my beloved, and this is my friend" (SOS 5:16, NKJV). I can remember the first time when I told Mandy that she was literally my best

friend in the world. There came a time in our relationship when I realized that I trusted her more explicitly than anyone else in my life, and that I wanted to go to her with everything, to share everything with her. To this day, I still believe and feel this way about Mandy. She is the person I want to have fun with. She is who I long to talk to about the normal happenings of the day, as well as my deepest fears and dreams.

Friendship is the bedrock of a lasting committed relationship. It is the foundation of dating, engagement, and marriage. When a builder begins to build a house, he does not start with the hardwood floor that everyone is excited about . . . no, he starts with the foundation. It would be ridiculous to start any other way, right? I think sometimes we are tempted, when we begin to be interested in someone, to skip the whole friendship aspect so that we can jump into the romantic stuff. This is not wise. The romantic feelings and actions will all fade at some time. When they do, if your relationship is founded upon them and not friendship, your relationship will begin to fade as well.

I am not saying that there is a set formula. I have two friends who were great friends for two years before they ever even thought about each other in romantic terms. I also have two other friends who just met, and are already interested in each other, and are using dating as a means to build their friendship. I do not think that either of these is wrong. I would say that I think the first is safer. It takes very mature people to be able to learn friendship through dating, and normally it is easier to become friends first, without the intensity of commitment that dating brings. It is also important to realize that if your whole relationship is founded on the presumption that you are romantically interested in each other, and not on true friendship— then if the romantic relationship ends, it will be nearly impossible to continue any kind of meaningful friendship.

My main point is: do not rush into commitment. You have plenty of time; allow your friendship to grow. This is difficult I know, especially when there is an immediate drawing of one person to the other, but seek God on how to honestly build friendship. Also, while you are dating, cultivate friendship and not just romance. It is important to talk, to "be real," to do fun things together. Be careful not to become immersed in serious commitment talks, kissing, and conversations about future and marriage. These can all be good, but if they begin to rule your relationship you will find the fiber of your connection to each other eroding quickly. Even now in marriage, if Mandy and I allow daily life to consume us for too long without connecting on a friendship basis, we feel distance creeping into our relationship. When that happens we know we need to just spend time together and enjoy each other as people. We need to remind ourselves that we are not only married, but we are friends.

Not Too Serious Too Fast

One way to ensure that this happens is to adhere to a principle of not getting too serious too fast. This is especially true for younger people. As teens and young adults, although it may be very tempting to rush quickly into a really deep and serious relationship, it is best often to make a conscious and concerted effort to take the relationship slowly. There is plenty of time to grow together and learn about each other. Give yourselves a chance to enjoy being together, having fun together, talking for long hours—without having to be wrapped up in the stuff of committed relationships. I know that may sound slightly contrary to the point of this book—but remember, I believe in balance. Dating is a good tool, but it needs to be used wisely.

I know a couple who were both 17 years old when they began to be interested in each other. After only a few weeks of their relationship, they each came to me asking for advice on how to know if this person was "the one." They were praying together about it, asking their parents about it, and now seeking pastoral counsel. Why does this even have to be an issue? After three weeks of two 17-year-olds dating, should marriage even be talked about? No way! You see, by doing this, they had completely halted their growth as friends and as a couple. They were trying to make a decision that is virtually impossible to make because neither one was ready to make it. They barely knew each other!

We need to be patient. Lust and infatuation both grow very, very quickly—and then fade almost as fast as they come. True love, on the other hand, grows steadily, slowly, over time. I am not saying you cannot "fall in love," or that you cannot have true love feelings for another person without knowing her for years. I am saying that we need to give love time to grow. We cannot force it or rush it. And rushing it will only stunt its growth.

Guard Your Heart

When entering into a relationship, keeping it from moving too quickly is very important, but perhaps the most important aspect of moving into a relationship is learning how to guard your heart. There is an incredibly telling verse in Proverbs 4:23,

Above all else, guard your heart, for it is the wellspring of life.

This principle is vital, but many people do not practice it. How I apply this verse to dating is this: in your heart are all the treasures of who you are—what makes up "you." These may include your dreams, your fears, your thoughts, your aspirations, your desires —both about the relationship, and about life in general. Many of us are tempted, because of romance, and our feeling that God wants us to be "honest," to pour out our hearts quickly and all the time. This verse however teaches something very different. You see, Solomon knew that we needed to jealously guard the treasures of our hearts, because out of our hearts flows our life. And while it is important to share your life with the person you are committing to in relationship, it is not necessary to reveal everything immediately.

I once knew a couple who felt the need to be extremely honest with each other all the time. These two did not know for sure that they were going to get married and in fact they did not—but they consistently revealed parts of their heart that are sacred. For instance, I remember talking to one of my friends after he had just told a girl that he was interested in her. After telling her this, he went on to tell her all his doubts about the potential relationship as well. He told her the reasons he had thought of that she might not work for him. And he told her all his doubts about her as a person, including some character flaws he saw in her. Those are very good things to be thinking about and pondering in your heart while getting to know someone seriously—Do I mesh well with this person? Do I like his/her attitude? What are his/her flaws? Can I live with his/her flaws? But to come out and reveal all those secret thoughts of the heart to someone else— that is like allowing someone to rob your heart! In that particular situation so much was revealed at the wrong time that they never recovered as a couple.

Be wise with the secret places of your heart, and do not divulge them for the sake of being honest. You can be honest without giving away all of your secrets immediately. There is a season of learning about each other and earning each other's trust that must occur before many parts of the heart can be shared. The Bible says three times in Song of Solomon—"Do not stir up nor awaken love until it pleases." This means that we need to allow our relationship to grow naturally, and follow wisdom before we open up the secrets of our hearts.

This principle of guarding your heart can feel a little abstract, and I greatly desire for you to understand it and be able to effectively apply it to your relationship. Following are several specific ways to measure how you are guarding your heart: (1) Honesty; (2) Saying "I love you;" (3) Using words that imply commitment; (4) Isolationism; and (5) Physical Intimacy.

The Power of Honesty

First, we can monitor the level of honesty we have, and the timing in which we choose to share openly. There is something profound and real about honesty. Honesty binds people together—it changes how two people feel about each other and how they relate to each other. I once heard it said that intimacy is something that is shared between you and one other person. There is a power in releasing something that is secret in your heart, out into the realm of another person's heart. That trust and vulnerability connect the two of you.

Jesus talks about going into a secret place when we pray, and our Father will see us in secret, and reward us openly (Matthew 6:6). This verse shows the intimacy of relationship that comes from honesty and the sharing of secrets. God did not want our prayers to be in front of everyone, to gain attention from all. He wanted them to be something shared only between us and the Lord—he wanted the intentions behind our prayers to be intimacy and closeness with God, not impressing other people. So he told us to go close the door behind us and pray in secret. Jesus understood the power of sharing the depths of our heart with another person.

The more vulnerable you become with someone, the stronger the tie between the two of you is. God wants us to be completely close to him—that is why he states in Matthew that the greatest commandment is to love our God with all our heart, soul, and mind (22:37). God does not desire from us a partial or reserved love—he wants all of us. He asks us to pour out our heart before him, to hold nothing back, to become completely vulnerable. The reason for this is that he loves us, and desires to have the most real and genuine relationship with us as possible.

I hope I have convinced you of this by now, that there is power in honesty to unite two people in a very strong way. The caution and wisdom we use is not to hurt the person we are in love with, but to protect both of us from becoming too close at the wrong time. Let me give you another example. After a long period of being friends and hanging out every day and night, Mandy and I finally decided to start dating officially. It was not until some time into that phase, that I felt released by God to share some mistakes from my past that I was not real happy about. This was a huge step for me, and I knew that to share this with her meant essentially saying I was very serious about this girl. I prayed over it for a long time, and then eventually shared my heart with her. I thought that the timing—the patience to wait until it was right—worked perfectly for us. And it served to draw us closer together at the right time, and not prematurely.

The Power of the Word "Love"

Another very practical step to make sure you are guarding your heart concerns the use of the word "love." You may think I am a stickler about this, but it is important. First of all, love is not just a feeling; it is a choice. There are feelings that go along with it, but in reality true love is a choice. This is a theme you will see throughout this book. If love was simply feeling attracted or infatuated or "in love," then not many people would stay married. Love is a choice to serve the other person no matter what happens.

When we say to someone, "I love you," this is not merely an expression of feelings; it is a commitment. It is saying, at some level, "I choose to love you and to commit my heart to you." Again, in saying this, much like with honesty, you are creating a bond that is powerful and must be dealt with carefully. In other words, you do not want to be telling every girl you think is pretty that you love her. Every time you start to get close to a girl or a boy romantically, do not blurt it out because the candle light is so romantic, and the music is so pretty, and she looks so good and...and . . and . . . . Hold onto "love." That is my theme. Treat it like it is very special, because it is. Your love should not be given out cheaply.

I can remember one day getting ready at my apartment for a date with Mandy. By this time, I was definitely "in love" with her. I had all the great feelings, the excitement when she called, the anticipation when I woke up every day that I might get to see her, the butterflies when she walked into the room, the wide-eyed wonder at how beautiful she was. . . you get the picture. This had been happening for some time now, but we had yet to say, "I love you" to each other. I remember very vividly being in the shower praying, crying out to God—"Do I love her? Can I say it?"

You see, I had treated these words with such reverence that it had been years since I had said them to any girl. I wanted to keep these words special. And I knew if I said them, I was really saying, "I don't know where this is going, but I want to commit to seeing it through because I think there is something here." So I prayed and prayed and when she came in that night, I sat her down very seriously and said in a solemn voice—"I feel like God has released me to say this, after much prayer and thought and more prayer. . . I think I love you." How romantic (ha!)! I was so serious it makes me laugh now!

Although I may have been a little over the top and too careful, the point still stands—saying, "I love you" to someone is a huge step. Do not take it lightly. Guard your heart and guard those words. Save them for when you truly mean them. I am not saying you can never say this to someone before you know you will marry them, only that you should know what you mean when you say it, and use it sparingly. It is a treasure of your heart that you do not want to be spilled out everywhere.

Don't Commit Until You Commit

Words that commit you to someone are equally as powerful as the words "I love you." Be careful in a relationship to not get caught up into romance so much, that you begin to make covenants that are impossible to keep. After breaking up with a girlfriend when I was sixteen, she said to me—"but you said you would always love me!" And I remember saying something lame back to her along the lines of, "I will always love you—just not as a girlfriend!" I was great with one-liners back then!

The point is I did make a commitment to her that was totally unrealistic. I told her I would love her forever, when in reality the only person you can say that to is your wife or husband! Many people want to say very romantic and meaningful phrases to promote falling in love even more, so we come up with all sorts of promises and statements like—"I will never leave you" or "I promise we are going to get married" or "We will be together forever" or "No one will ever come between us!" These all sound great, but realistically they can only be said once you make the real commitment—"I do!" With Mandy, I never said anything like those statements for two and half years (and believe me I wanted to) until we were engaged. Only then did I feel I could make those promises and keep them.

Again, guard your heart. Do not give away these promises of your heart until you are really in a position to do so. Try to steer away from promises and most sentences that end in "forever" until you are ready to make good on them.

Be Careful Of Isolationism

Have you ever had a friend who once she or he started dating someone, simply disappeared from your life? This is one danger of dating. I think to some extent this is healthy and normal, because two people who are in love are supposed to spend a lot of time together. However, when the time spent together becomes unreasonable and begins to damage other important friendships in your life, you need to change.

I have seen two people become so wrapped up in each other that they both lose their individual identities. Even in marriage, where two actually do become one, it is important to maintain individuality so that each person can bless and strengthen the other. So much more in dating then, it is important for you to keep your individual life. If you find that you never have time for your other friends, or you have to take your partner with you everywhere, or you begin to lose or forget goals and dreams that you as an individual have in life—then you may want to re-think how much time the two of you are spending with one another. Time is also a very powerful force, and spending lots of time together creates a powerful bond. Before marriage, it is crucial to maintain your individuality. Some people want to be married, or at least act married, so badly that they create a pseudo-married relationship within their dating relationship. What I mean is they act like they are married (but not in a healthy way) and do not allow themselves the freedom they should.

My basic point is this: it is important to keep your own life separate from your partner while you are dating. This is important because it brings balance to your life, it brings perspective and objectivity to your relationship, and it helps each of you to evaluate and understand your relationship better. If all you know is your relationship (if you become isolated and only spend time with each other) then it will be difficult to ever see when change needs to happen. Maintaining outside friendship relationships can give you the tie to the "real world" that is so crucial as you try to discover God's plan for your future together. You need other people's eyes and ears—people need to see and hear your relationship—people you trust who can speak into your life and give you advice. This perspective allows for more growth and a healthier understanding of where God is taking you.

The Power of Physical Intimacy
This last point is so important that I needed to commit an entire chapter to it (Chapter 6). Physical intimacy, like nothing else, creates a very strong bond between two people. The further you allow yourselves to go physically, the greater the bond. And these bonds are real. So be careful with how you handle this area of relationships, and please read the next chapter on physical holiness for more in depth insight on the power of this kind of intimacy.

Prayer
Besides guarding your heart, another very important aspect of beginning a relationship is constantly saturating it in prayer. The following scriptures were (and continue to be) fundamental in my commitment to following God's plan for my life and my relationship with Mandy:

Trust in the Lord with all your heart and lean not on your
own understanding; in all your ways acknowledge him, and
he will make your paths straight (Proverbs 3:5-6).

Commit your way to the Lord, trust also in Him, and He
shall bring it to pass (Psalm 37:5, NKJV).

When I say prayer, I am not thinking of praying as a couple, although
that can be good too; I am mostly referring to prayer on your own. Prayer
that is between you and God about the relationship, and about your
partner. One difficulty in a dating relationship is keeping your distance,
while wanting to be so close. You must realize however that you are not yet
married. You both go home to your separate homes, and this is always a good
time to remember you have separate lives. Although you have begun to join
your lives together, you are not permanently joined. And this is important
to remember because it allows you the freedom to analyze, scrutinize, and
pray over your relationship and about your partner. Once you are married
you cannot ask God, "Should I be married to this person, is this really the
one?" because the answer is yes. But before you are married you should not
feel like you are betraying your boyfriend or girlfriend by raising questions
and doubts to God. In fact, dating is the time you should raise all these
questions and doubts.

That is so important. Almost every day for a couple years of dating
I lifted my heart to God and asked for his guidance, asked for his wisdom,
asked for him to show us his plan, and asked for him to grow us together or
apart from each other. I wanted his will alone. Regardless of how strong
my feelings for Mandy were, I wanted to know this was God's plan above
all else. So I encourage you to pray on a regular basis for each other, and to
pray for God to show your heart—individually and independently of your
partner—what his plan is for you in the relationship, as well as his plan for
the two of you.

Small Group Discussion Questions:
It is human nature to want to rush into things. What are some reasons, in your opinion, that people start dating too quickly?

What are some of the consequences of starting too fast?

Have you ever been tempted to skip the friendship stage of a relationship and jump right into a romantic relationship? What was the outcome?

What dangers exist when friendship is not the foundation of a romantic relationship?

Which of the ways in which people do not guard their heart (too much honesty, saying 'I love you' too soon, using 'commitment' words, isolationism, and physical intimacy) is, or would be, the most tempting for you and why?

The Bible says in three places to "not awaken love before it pleases." What do you think that means?

Why is it important (especially in the beginning stages of dating) to continue to examine one another critically? Does that sound unromantic to you? Do you think it is unloving to be critical of each other?

If you have been in a dating relationship before, how often did you pray about it while you were dating? How often did you seek God for direction and clarity about the other person?

What are some things you can be praying about individually while in a dating relationship?

Do you think it is a good idea or a bad idea to pray together early in a dating relationship?

How far is too far?

How to set boundaries, and stick to them

This is a difficult chapter to write. Where will most people reading this book be coming from? What background of beliefs will they hold? There is a vast spectrum from which you could be approaching this book, and this chapter in particular. Just looking at today's culture, we can see the polarization. The secular arena seems to be encouraging more sex with more people, the Christian population seems to be running for cover and telling their children to not look at the opposite sex until they have that wedding ring!

The limits and boundaries of physical intimacy in "dating" relationships is a topic that most teenagers and young adults debate. People often ask me about kissing and what limits there should be for physical contact. When can we kiss? How often? Can we kiss at all? In this chapter I want to have an honest discussion about physical intimacy and sin. I am not going to be arguing that everyone should stay away from all forms of physical contact until they are married. This is dangerous ground I know. There are many people in modern Christianity who believe that everything (kissing, hugging, holding hands) should be saved for marriage, and that to do anything else is betraying your future spouse. I do not hold that conviction—nonetheless, what I have to share in this chapter is profitable for people coming from any perspective. If you have decided to hold off on all physical contact until marriage, the principles I will discuss in this chapter are still vital for your success. And if you are already, or are planning on, having physical contact with your boyfriend or girlfriend, then the guidelines I put forth in this chapter will also be crucial for you to maintain your physical holiness.

What I am writing here is not popular in much of Christianity. I can hear many parents and youth pastors getting upset with me even as I type. Many would question me—"If you admit that physical contact could lead to sin, then why not just write about completely staying away from it?" This line of thinking, however, serves more to avoid the problems of physical holiness, than to honestly deal with them. And furthermore, there are all sorts of activities that could easily lead to sin (driving could lead to speeding; talking could lead to gossip) but we do not stay away from them because they are not inherently evil. The simple fact that something could lead to sin does not mean it must—nor that it will. And I think that to brush the whole problem aside by telling you to stay away from everything physical would be easy for me, but not be very much help to you.

There is an old adage that says—"if you give a man a fish, he will eat for a day; but if you teach a man to fish, he will eat for a lifetime." If I were to simply tell you, "All physical contact is bad and unholy and you should not do anything until you are married," and then send you off into your relationship, I would have failed you. I know only a few who have never kissed until they were married, and I honor them—that is awesome and I think it is great. But the reality is, most people have either already begun kissing or more in their relationships, or they plan to because they do not think it is wrong. So what I want to do is teach you how to fish (so to speak) instead of just giving you the fish of "Don't do anything." Instead of avoiding the topic, I want to deal with it. I want to teach you how to go from where you are now and live holy within your relationship.

One last caveat before I begin: Jesus said some very strong stuff about people who make his children stumble (something about cinderblocks and lots of water). So I do not want the following words in this chapter to in any way give anyone license to sin. As you read you may discover that my boundaries are less strict than yours. If this is the case, please do not throw away your convictions. If God has given you personal convictions that go further than mine, that's great. Please honor what the Lord has put in your heart. Decisions for your relationship are ultimately yours, and you are responsible before God for your decisions. Many people, however, will have looser boundaries than mine. I encourage you to prayerfully consider the following boundaries, as I found them invaluable in keeping me holy while I was dating Mandy.

It Starts With An Attitude

The basic question that people ask when talking about this issue is "How far can we go?" How much physical intimacy is too much? When I was 15 years old, I used to love to find books about dating. Of course, I would turn immediately to the chapter on physical intimacy. This is somewhat embarrassing to share, but for some reason (note the sarcasm) I always seemed to agree most with the authors that said I could do more! My attitude was more along the lines of trying to see how much I could get away with, than truly wanting to know God's limits.

This is an attitude that flies right in the face of true holiness and purity; however we see it in our lives every day. We are constantly trying to rationalize "smaller" sins—or looking for "gray" areas about which the Bible seems silent. We see rationalization come on the scene of humanity in the first temptation recorded in mankind! When the serpent tempts Eve in Genesis 3, he tells her that this fruit is indeed not going to kill her—but that instead it will give her wisdom! In verse 6, Eve's thinking process is recorded,

> When the woman saw that the fruit of the tree was good for food, and also desirable for gaining wisdom, she took some and ate it (Gen 3:6).

Although it says that she saw the fruit "was good for food," it was not simply for culinary reasons that she grabbed it. There was plenty of other great food to be eaten. Certainly the desire to eat would not be strong enough to forego God's warning. What led her over the edge, though, was that even though it was wrong, there was an upside. I can hear myself in this situation—"Well God wants to give me the desires of my heart, right? And he says if I ask for wisdom he will give it to me. Surely he didn't mean for me not to be able to gain wisdom from this . . .I'm just being legalistic about the whole thing. . ." And if I follow that thinking, then I use my powers of rationalization to make a decision that my heart knows is against God's will —just as Eve did.

Be honest—have you ever been down that path? This same thinking happens when thinking about physical intimacy. Let's say you begin by holding hands and kissing. At some point your desire is to do more—to try something new. You begin to think thoughts like, "I love her. I know the Bible talks strongly against lust and sexual immorality, but if I love her, can it really be lust? I mean, Paul told us that "everything is permissible for me—but not everything is beneficial" (1 Cor. 6:12). Well this certainly is not going to harm us in anyway—in fact—it will most likely bring us closer as a couple. So it must be OK if I love her . . ."

The attitude behind this, and many forms of sin, is an attitude of trying to get as close to sin as possible, without actually sinning. This is crazy logic. Apply that logic to something like murder—"How much can I murder this person, without actually murdering them?" That is impossible! For some reason when it comes to lust and sexual sin, we feel we can walk the tightrope, balancing as close to the pit of sin as possible without actually falling in. Is this how we should, or even want to, live our lives?

I Corinthians 6:18 tells us to "flee from sexual immorality." To flee does not mean "to get as close to as possible without actually touching it" does it? No! It means to run from—to hide from—to do everything within one's power to escape. This is the attitude I am talking about. It is an attitude of no compromise, of understanding that "gray" areas are most often darkness in disguise. It is an attitude of honesty with yourself. It calls for being willing to truly examine your motivations, your thoughts—the "inward man."

Jesus taught this attitude as well. When teaching about adultery he did not follow the letter of the law, but rather enforced the spirit of it, saying that even to look at a woman with desire or covetousness is equivalent to adultery. He took the law and made it a heart matter. This is such a powerful understanding.

In Jeremiah 31:33 God said he wanted to take his people and put his "law in their minds, and write it on their hearts." The law of the Old Testament was a law that was outside of our hearts. It was an external motivator—Paul calls it a Tutor in Galatians 3. A tutor is someone outside of us that forces us to comply with a standard. However God did not simply want obedience to external regulations and the threat of punishment. He wanted obedience that came from the inside, motivated internally by love for Jesus. That is what Jesus was talking about when he took obvious laws and made them apply to the heart. Jesus did not want us to be going into situations and saying, "Hold everything! Let me see if there is a commandment in the Bible that explicitly deals with this situation." He wanted us instead to be "transformed by the renewing of your mind" (Rom 12:2) so that we could, in every situation, know God's will! He wanted us to become lovers of what is good and upright, not simply machines doing what we have been told.

So when it comes to physical intimacy in a relationship before you are married, become a lover of what is good. Become a lover of what is godly and pure. So that when you are (and you will be) confronted with a situation in which you are tempted to hedge and rationalize because you love each other SO much—you will not have to ask "Why didn't God say something specific in the Bible about this?" You will rather be able to "test and approve" (Rom 12:2) what God's will is, by simply knowing Him and having his law written in your heart, instead of on some paper (or stone tablet) in front of you. And cultivate an attitude of then fleeing from everything that is not good and godly, rather than trying to get away with as much as possible.

Everything You Do Together Is Special

It is important to understand that even holding hands is incredibly special. Some people seem to miss this point and think that the goal of all physical contact is sex. That is simply not so. Even now that I am married, and we can do whatever we want, holding hands with Mandy is still awesome! I cannot tell you how much I love to walk down Main Street in my hometown holding Mandy's hand. It is something so powerful and so special. I am serious! And building this understanding into your relationship will produce an incredible effect.

Do not take holding hands, hugging, and goodnight kisses on the cheek for granted—there is meaning and love communicated in all of these. So you should not be just willing to give these out to any old boyfriend or girlfriend. I am serious! Guard these! They are beautiful and wonderful gifts to someone you love. When I was dating Mandy, she refused to go out to dinner with me until we were really serious (until we both had said "I love you"—and that took a while!) because to her, that was very special. That is what I am talking about. Understand that certain aspects of romantic relationships are very special and should be shared sparingly.

I am not saying you should only hold hands with someone when you have received the word from God that this person is "the one." For some out there, that may be necessary—but not for most. What I am saying is to not go holding hands and kissing every boy or girl that says you look nice. Or even every potentially serious love interest. Wait until there is some substantial commitment on both sides to finding out where the relationship is going.

Set Parameters Together!

I am not going to tell you what you can do. But I am going to tell you what you certainly cannot do. I think the rest is a decision that needs to be made by both of you in the relationship, along with guidance from your parents and other spiritual leaders in your life. I encourage you to be open and honest about physical intimacy with each other, and with older more mature people in your lives. This is the worst area in which to become isolated, but often the easiest as well. So work hard to keep this area of your relationship in the light. Part of doing that is setting specific boundaries and sticking to them.

Prepare yourself, I am about to talk a little graphically. It is easy to gloss over this stuff—but I wish that someone had been straight up with me about this kind of stuff when I was younger. There are many teenagers and young adults out there who are looking for specific parameters from the Bible. I recently watched a "Dateline" special about sex and teenagers. They were talking to teens (even young teens around 13 years old) about oral sex like it was an everyday occurrence. If this is what the world is talking about, then it is what the church needs to address as well.

Does the Bible deal with any of this specifically? Yes. And as a Christian you should know why it is you don't do this stuff. So I want to give you an explicit verse from the Bible that helped me a lot. The Bible, in Ezekiel 23:3,21 teaches us by implication that to touch the breast of a girl whom you are not married to is very wrong and against God's will (read it if you do not believe me). The author equates this act to the ungodly pillaging of Israel. So for me, when I was dating —kissing, holding hands, and hugging were the only things I was allowed to do because the Bible does not forbid them. Everything else is totally off limits. Everything else is sinful. It is not a gray area, but a definite, certain, and complete reality —it is wrong. It is impure and lustful. So stay away from it!

The discussion does not end there. Kissing is a very complicated issue. The main question to ask yourself is, "what does kissing do to you?" Does it depend on the kind of kissing? On what kind of situations? For instance, kissing lying down on the couch can be much more dangerous than kissing standing up. And being alone in a house can be much more tempting than being alone in the family room, while your parents are in a nearby room.

What I am getting at is this—you need to decide some guidelines, some parameters that protect you. Some people, I believe, can kiss alone in a room without being tempted to do more. However, some people cannot hold hands without their minds racing into places they should not be. You and your partner need to be honest with one another—and the parameters need to be set to protect the weaker of the two of you. You have to approach this with tenacity in your desire to not sin, or else you will fall into temptation.

In my relationship with Mandy, before any physical contact came into the picture for us, we openly talked over what each of us thought was right and wrong for us to do. We then made rules based on whose convictions were the strictest. This is so important. Even if you are not going to kiss until you get married, it is important to discuss that. Why? Because when you openly discuss parameters, then they are brought into the light. 1 John 1:5 says that "God is light; in Him there is no darkness at all." If you don't discuss this topic—if you leave it in the dark—you have left an enormous door open for the Enemy to tempt you, even if you plan on not kissing or touching at all!

Think about it—when should you make a decision regarding something physical—while you are passionately looking one another in the eyes or while you are rationally discussing what God's will is? I think the choice is clear. The other great aspect in this process is that once you bring it into the light, you both then become accountable for abiding by those parameters. Ecclesiastes 4:9-10 reads,

> Two are better than one, because they have a good return
> for their work: If one falls down, his friend can help him up.
> But pity the man who falls and has no one to help him up!

If you have never talked over your boundaries as a couple, then you will never know if one is struggling, weak, or being tempted to break one of them. You are both essentially alone in your struggle to stay pure. If you both know, however, and are praying and working together to stay holy as a couple, then most often when one is weak, the other will be strong, and no one will fall. You can take this principle and apply it to accountability relationships as well. Two couples are also stronger than one. It is crucial to have accountability to other people when you are dating, especially in the physical aspect of the relationship.

This principle of two being stronger than one, and the importance of setting guidelines gets more important the further into the relationship you go. If you think temptation is difficult in the first six months of a relationship . . . wait until you are engaged. Every couple that I have been close to over the past five years that has gone from dating, into engagement, and into marriage, have renegotiated their guidelines the closer they got to the actual wedding. You cannot just set parameters once and live by them—you have to continually adjust them.

If You Have Decided That Kissing Is OK . . .

If, in setting your parameters, the two of you have come to the conclusion that kissing will be allowed in your relationship—or if you are not yet with someone, but believe it is ok and plan on kissing in the future before you get married, I want to give you two extra tips. Again, for many I am sure this is frustrating to read, because you are saying, "Just don't kiss at all!" But I will re-assert what I said earlier: My goal here is to help as many as possible. And from my experience, there are many people out there who feel that kissing is OK. I do not want to leave all those people stranded (and in fact I was included in that group when I dated) so I want to tell them what I have learned.

First—please keep kissing a very special thing. When I was younger (I am being brutally honest about myself in this chapter!) I had one relationship in which I regret ever kissing this person. At the time I was too immature and misguided to understand the "specialness" of kissing, and I gave that gift to someone I should not have. For the rest of my non-married years though, I strongly adhered to an understanding that I would not kiss just anyone. I set up guidelines for when I would allow myself to kiss someone. My guidelines were simple: 1) I could not kiss anyone if I could not say to them "I love you" and mean it (this is huge for me—"I love you" is so sacred that it truly cannot be doled out to many people honestly in your life) and 2) I had to be seriously committed to this person, and to seeing where the relationship would go—with the definite possibility in my mind that this could end up in marriage. If I didn't think we could get married, I had no business dating at all!

So those were my guidelines, you need to figure out your own, but be careful—do not give this away easily. Second, do not allow kissing to become your whole relationship. Seriously. For many couples, once they start kissing, it takes over their relationship. Kissing and physical contact cannot become the crux of your relationship, or else your relationship will die. It should be a small percentage compared to the talking, sharing, and having fun that you do. If you have a hard time with this, then you need to either discipline yourselves to only kissing a certain amount of time, or if it totally overwhelms you both, then throw it out all together.

Lastly I want to make a few very practical points. I said this earlier but I want to reiterate: kissing in the dark is more tempting than kissing with a light on; kissing lying down is more tempting than while standing up; kissing alone in a house is more tempting than if there are other people there; kissing in a bedroom is much more tempting than any other room of the house; and kissing too late at night is much more tempting than earlier in the day. I am not going to make these rules for you, but you need to be wise and you need to flee from sin, remember? Kissing at 1am in your girlfriend's bedroom, while lying down watching a movie is something you should avoid. I know as Mandy and I got closer and closer we had to set stricter boundaries, and many of them concerned the details I just mentioned. I know a couple who actually would not allow themselves to kiss past a certain time of night, because it just became too tempting to go further.

One more practical insight is about the rest of your body while you are kissing. I am trying to be as forthright as possible here —what are your hands doing while you are kissing? What is your body doing? If you are kissing and moving your bodies together imitating sex, then you are sinning. Plain as that. Call it sin. Decide not to do it anymore. I have found that this is the "good-Christian-sin" of dating. People somehow are able to excuse this, but it is very dangerous and very sinful. So, honestly, don't do it. Flee from it.

Become Accountable

The next step after setting parameters is being accountable to keep them. While it is very important to create these guidelines together so that two can be stronger than one—in relationships more than two is needed. This is where accountability to outside sources is invaluable. James 5:16 says to "confess your sins to each other and pray for each other so that you may be healed." This is accountability—not being afraid to share your victories and your struggles with people whom you trust, and who will commit to pray for you so that you may be freed from any sin.

There are two kinds of accountability that I see happening in a committed and serious relationship. The first level is individual. Each person is responsible to their partner and to God to become personally accountable while in a relationship. I think, in fact, that accountability on a regular basis is something that all Christians should have regardless of being in a relationship, but once you are in one, this becomes even more crucial. You each should have people to tell about your physical temptations, your fears, and even your doubts. When it comes to temptation, these people can be a spur to holiness in your life through prayer and "checking up" on you. Concerning doubts and fear, these people can serve as a sounding board to help you as you wade through your feelings and thoughts.

Be wise in choosing people with whom you will be accountable. In Matthew 7:6 Jesus said,

> Do not give what is holy to the dogs; nor cast your pearls
> before swine, lest they trample them under their feet, and
> turn and tear you to pieces.

The secrets of your heart—your weaknesses, doubts, fears, and dreams—these are holy. It is not wise to open your heart to just anyone, lest they "turn and tear you to pieces." You need to find people you trust, people who are willing to pray for you, and people you look up to in some way. I have found that mature friends, trusted adults, and parents are all good sources for many of these forms of accountability. But be sure to choose people who are mature and capable of filling this role in your life. Lastly, if you are becoming accountable to someone for temptation in your life or relationship, be sure they are for the most part free from struggle in that area personally. For instance, if you struggle with drinking excessively, and you ask your friend who is an alcoholic to help keep you accountable, that was probably not the wisest choice you could have made.

The second form of accountability is for the couple. I would counsel you, as a couple, to first look for other (often older, but not always) couples who display characteristics or qualities in their relationship that you would hope to emulate. It is good to watch those couples and learn from them. It is also very powerful, though, to find one or two that fit that category and ask them to mentor you in some way. This can be an invaluable resource of wisdom, counsel, and accountability. As you begin to share your hearts with this couple, they will not only be able to keep you accountable physically, but also emotionally and mentally as well.

While accountability may be scary and very vulnerable, I have found it is maybe the most effective tool against sin. God created the body of Christ to need one another (1 Corinthians 13) so it behooves us to rely on one another in healthy, trusting relationships. It is worth the difficulty to stay pure as a couple.

Freedom From The Past

Some of you, while reading this chapter, may have realized that what you are doing in your relationship currently (or have done in the past) is wrong. You have felt the twinge of conviction from the Holy Spirit, but at the same time your defenses have gone up, trying to ward off guilt and condemnation by proclaiming—"We have tried to stop and we cannot, so leave me alone!" I want to say to you that you can stop.

But first I want to tell you that no matter what has been done, the

Bible teaches us "therefore, there is now no condemnation for those who are in Christ Jesus" (Romans 8:1). God's love and acceptance for you is truly not based on what you have done but on who you are—his child. This is not a license to sin, but it is the door to true relationship with him which will in turn free you from sin. The enemy, when it comes to sin, tries to win twice with us. First he tempts us, then if we fall, he changes his tune and begins to scold us for sinning, making us feel guilty. If you have been beaten once, do not allow him to get the second victory! When we sin we are called to true remorse and sorrow:

> Godly sorrow brings repentance that leads to salvation and
> leaves no regret, but worldly sorrow brings death.
> (2 Corinthians 7:10)

However, we are called to the sorrow that leads us to Jesus, not a week-long guilt trip.

With that understanding in our hearts, that we do not need to live under condemnation, I want to share with you two very important verses in regards to sin. First is 1 John 1:9,

> If we confess our sins, he is faithful and just and will forgive
> us our sins and purify us from all unrighteousness.

If, by reading part of this book, you have come to the realization that you are living, or have lived, outside the will of God for your physical relationship, the first step is confession and repentance. Confession is powerful because it is calling sin what it is—it forces you to bring this thing into the light and not allow it to hide in the darkness any longer. Once we have done this, the scripture tells us that Jesus forgives us and cleanses us. We no longer have need for guilt or beating ourselves up, but now we must move into repentance—which means to turn away from the sin. The second verse I want to share deals with this aspect—Romans 6:14,

> For sin shall not have dominion over you, for you are not
> under the law but under grace (NKJV).

This is a promise from God to you. Sin will not rule you. "Because through Christ Jesus the law of the Spirit of life set me free from the law of sin and death." (Romans 8:2). You have been set free. I know what it feels like to feel that a certain sin area is unconquerable. But in reality, there is no sin that God cannot free us from. Remember: in every temptation God makes a way of escape (1 Corinthians 10:13). Your job is to find that. For many of you, strict and honest accountability is the answer. For others—tougher guidelines for yourself. And for all of us—fostering a more genuine and life-changing relationship with Jesus is the best defense against sin.

I wish I could talk to you and let you know that even now it is worth stopping. You may wonder, especially if you have had sex, "What is the point of stopping now, I already messed up?" And this is what I would say—God is a God of redemption. He always has been. He wants to redeem your relationship. What that means is he wants to take what was meant for bad, and make it for good. He promises to do that in Romans 8:28—"in all things God works for the good of those who love him." Also, think of your premarital relationship in these terms—you are sowing seed that will be reaped in marriage. You can decide to sow seeds of sin that will be reaped as problems in your marriage, or seeds of obedience that will be reaped as life. And the Lord is faithful to reward you, even if you have stumbled up to this point—God wants you now. He is ready to forget the past and press on to the future for your relationship. So decide today, I encourage you, to walk in holiness from here on out. God is on your side—he always has been. And by his strength you can overcome this, and he will bring a blessing in your life and relationship as a result.

Worship The Lord In The Beauty Of Holiness (Psalm 29:2, NKJV)
Sin opens the door to more sin in other areas of your relationship. And physical purity is one of the first places the enemy will challenge you as a couple. Whether you decide to not hold hands until you are married, or that kissing is ok—Satan desires to make you stumble. Do not let him.

> Be self-controlled and alert. Your enemy the devil prowls around like a roaring lion looking for someone to devour (1 Peter 5:8).

That verse is essentially what I am trying to convey in this chapter. Be on the alert. You have received fair warning that this testing is going to occur. Make yourselves ready. As a couple it is easy to become lax concerning physical holiness because you can easily get caught up in the intense and passionate feelings you have for one another. So do what is necessary to ensure that does not happen. Keep this area of your relationship totally in the light, before both of you and before others as well. Do not give the enemy or your flesh an inch through compromise, because he will not stop there! He wants to devour you! So you must resist him with the ferocity we talked about in the beginning of this chapter. Approach this holiness with tenacity—an attitude of, "I refuse to allow our physical holiness to be corrupted!" And with God's grace, he will lead you into purity and honesty that will be fertile ground for a wonderful future.

Small Group Discussion Questions:
Some Christians argue that premarital sex, or doing everything up to that, is permitted. What is your response to that? Do you think this is okay? Why or why not?

How far is too far in your opinion?

If we don't believe that crossing certain boundaries is "sin" how will we be able to resist crossing them?

Let's set some parameters. Whether you are in a relationship now or not, take some time to write down some rules about what you will (or would) allow physically in your relationship.

Can you think of some ideas for how to stick to those rules?

Do you know any couples who have successfully remained pure during their dating years?

Christian talks about accountability. If you are dating (or if you were to start dating in the future) write down a couple of people (or couples) with whom you would feel comfortable being accountable.

Most of us have things from our past in this area that we regret. If you have areas like this, are you able to feel God's forgiveness in them? Do you struggle with feeling condemned or unworthy because of past mistakes?

Looking forward to your future wedding night, what do you want to be able to offer to your spouse physically that you've shared with no one else ever before (including them)?

It is a sacrifice to remain pure through the years of dating. Is it worth it? Why?

[7]

How should we treat each other?

Not settling for anything but God's best

Have you ever received that "perfect" gift? You know, the gift that was timed just right and was exactly what you wanted? A perfect gift is both meaningful and practical at the same time. This example seems a little silly, but Mandy gave me one of these when we were engaged. For Christmas she bought me a gaming system. Now, maybe that sounds a little strange to you. A gaming system doesn't sound romantic and meaningful to many people, but she knew me. She knew I had never had one in my entire life. She knew how special this would be. So it was a perfect combination of meaningfulness and also usefulness—I loved it!

I know that I agonize over buying gifts, because I so badly want my gift to be the best ever. Well, this idea also applies to dating, and specifically to God. God wants you to have a perfect gift in your eventual spouse. He is excited about giving you to each other, and he knows how meaningful and powerful it will be. I call this the "good and perfect principle." He loves to give good gifts like I do! But sometimes we stand in the way of his gifts. Sometimes we settle for less than the perfect gift of God in our lives, and that is what this chapter is about. I am going to focus on (1) keeping your relationship emotionally righteous (so it remains a good gift), and (2) knowing when your partner or yourself is moving into unrighteousness.

The meaning of the word "righteous", in a very simple form, is to be right. When applied to Christianity, it means to be "right" according to God's standards. I chose this word to describe what I am talking about here because I have seen so many people in relationships where they are simply not treated "right." And there is no other way to put it. They are not being treated the way God would want them to be treated, in that good and perfect way. I have seen manipulation, pressure, intimidation, and many other forms of using the "love" in a romantic relationship to hurt someone. What I want to write about in this chapter is some guidelines for what is right—and why.

Many people who are in these sorts of relationships sadly are not even aware that they are being mistreated. They are blinded by their feelings in part, but I believe often they are victims of bad doctrine. I think many people have a misunderstanding of God's love and provision for them, and because of that they have grown to expect little or nothing from God's hand. There are even teachings out there like "seek his face and not his hand" that discourage having an expectation from God. However, I believe in Scripture God commands us to both seek his face and his hand. In fact we are reprimanded in James for not seeking his hand—"you do not have because you do not ask."

I think for many there is a fundamental belief that God is not to be bothered, and that he has more important things to do. For others, I believe we are so unable to receive God's forgiveness (or forgive ourselves) that we refuse to believe anything good will ever happen to us. Lastly, I think there are some who have been so wounded by others in their past that they are simply unable to even conceptualize something better existing, without the Lord healing them. With this in mind, I want to begin the chapter with a brief discussion of what I believe to be a correct view of God's love and provision in our lives. If we can lay the foundation that God loves us and intends good things for our lives, then we can begin to examine our relationships from a more "right" perspective.

Learn to Let God Love You—Become a Child of God

There is a deception that the Enemy tries to bring against God's children and it angers me whenever I hear it or see it. I see so many people who know in their head that God loves them, but do not truly believe it, experience it, or live it. Many times, as Christians, we get so caught up in trying to earn God's favor and love, that we forget to simply receive it. God is not a God who demands obedience before love. He says that out of true love will flow obedience. He says that he is looking not for sacrifice, but for contrite hearts. God is so in love with his people that he gave his only Son, the greatest gift to mankind ever. This is the love that God has for his children—however, in our realities, we often experience a very different God.

I just received an email from a friend and she was sharing with me about how she seems to only attract guys who are mean to her and want to take advantage of her physically. The weird thing is, and she admits this herself, that she continues to go back to these guys seeking attention. In fact one time when I was talking to her she actually began to blame herself for some of it. Today, as I was thinking about her situation, I remembered one time when I gave a teaching about God's love for us. She raised her hand when I asked for questions, and simply asked—"How can God love us? I mean, I know it in my head that the Bible says this, but I don't really understand it?" And now this is all beginning to make sense for me—the main reason she cannot find a guy who treats her right is that she does not even believe that God will treat her right—how can she expect more from a guy?

You see, she is a classic example of what I have been seeing more and more of as I travel around the east coast visiting and ministering to churches—there are so many Christians out there who know in their head that God loves them, but they do not truly believe it. And the reason it is important for me to discuss this is that these things are like building blocks—if you cannot believe God truly loves you, regardless of your sin, then you cannot believe that he wants to give you good and perfect gifts. And if you don't believe that principle, you will not expect good things in your life. And if you do not expect good things in your life, chances are . . . .

So, please listen to me with your heart. God, please open our hearts to hear your word in a way that penetrates through our faulty belief systems. There is a powerful verse in Galatians:

> So you are no longer a slave, but a son; and since you are a
> son, God has made you also an heir (4:7).

So many Christians do not live this verse. Sometimes when I talk to Christians I begin to feel that there are more slaves out there than children. Do you know what I mean?

I see Christians who are living mostly in what some call a "slave mentality." Their Christianity is dominated by guilt—either guilt for sin they have committed in the past, or guilt that they are not doing enough for

God. Therefore they are constantly trying to earn—to earn God's favor, forgiveness, love, appreciation—through doing good. However it is never enough. Many people are enslaved to this mentality because they were never shown love as children from their parents, and now they continue on in that—not expecting God to ever love them, unless they perform well. They live their lives feeling unworthy, inferior, unaccepted, and unappreciated by God.

But God is calling us out of slavery and into sonship and daughtership. You see God shows us in Romans 8:15 that we have not received "a spirit that makes you a slave again to fear, but you received the Spirit of sonship." God wants us as his children—he died to get us into his family. A huge part of breaking this misunderstanding, and beginning to live as a son or a daughter, is to truly know God's love. If you read through 1 Corinthians 13, put God's name in the place of love and read it to yourself. God is patient with you. God keeps no record of wrongs. God is not self-seeking, which means he is always seeking your good. God always trusts—he believes in you. If he did not believe in you and your abilities and gifts, he would not trust you—but he does. He believes in you and is proud of you!

There are three false beliefs (which I have seen a lot of—there may be more) that arise from not truly knowing God's love for us, and not understanding what it means to be a child of God. The first belief is not believing that God will answer your prayers and not believing that God wants to give you "good and perfect" gifts. The second is the belief that we must do good things to earn God's love. And the third belief is that we must continue to punish ourselves for our past sins. All of these have ramifications on dating, and I want to discuss each briefly:

False Belief #1
I Will Have to Settle
Specifically when it comes to dating, I think that many of us struggle with fearing that we will have to "settle" for someone who is not everything we had hoped for; fearing that no one will ever come or that God will call us to celibacy; or fearing that we will pick someone and later find out that we completely missed God's will and he will never bless our marriage. These fears are all deceptions and not at all like the God we see in the Bible.

I have heard my friends talking about their frustrations in finding a wife or husband. I have heard some say on occasion that "maybe God just wants me to marry that person—they are as close to what I am looking for as I can seem to find—maybe that's God's will and I am just being too picky."

Or "maybe God is going to call me to marry someone who is not everything I had hoped for, maybe I am being unrealistic." Granted, as I wrote earlier in the book, we have to understand that we will, in the end, marry a human. And humans are imperfect—therefore, if you have in mind an ideal that is impossible to take on human form, you will be let down. However, God wants to provide for us someone who truly "ravishes our heart."

This is the kind of gift that God gives. Without variation God gives gifts that are good (both outwardly and inwardly) that produce benefits, and that are perfect, mature, and whole. I picture it like this—if God were to walk up to you and hand you a present on your birthday, it would not be dented and dirty, with the paper ripped off, and the contents broken to pieces. God would give you a gift that looked perfect, was beautifully wrapped, and what is more—it not only would look perfect, but the actual gift would be the perfect gift. What makes a gift good? Its timeliness? Its special-ness to the person? Its meaning? God would have all of these taken care of.

Therefore, when you are thinking about your eventual spouse and worrying that God will not give you a good gift, or when you are in a relationship and not being treated righteously, remember the "good and perfect" principle. God desires, in fact longs, to give you a perfect gift. Anything less would be un-Godlike. He wants to bless you. He wants to give you someone who is good and perfect for you. Sometimes we fear we will have to settle for less than we want, that we should overlook serious flaws because we do not deserve better, but that is simply not true. The only reason we will have to settle is if we make that choice on our own—it will not be on account of God's gift. If you feel like you are settling, then maybe you have not found God's gift!

Read Jesus' words from the Sermon on the Mount in Matthew 7:7-11:

> Ask and it will be given to you; seek and you will find;
> knock and the door will be opened to you. For everyone
> who asks receives; he who seeks finds; and to him who
> knocks, the door will be opened. Which of you, if his son
> asks for bread, will give him a stone? Or if he asks for a fish,
> will give him a snake? If you, then, though you are evil,
> know how to give good gifts to your children, *how much*
> *more will your Father in heaven give good gifts to those who ask*
> *him!* (emphasis mine).

Do you see the principle here? God is not interested in giving us second-class gifts. It says in 1 John 3:1 that we are children of God. As our father, he is motivated by love to give us gifts that any parent would want for their children—gifts that are good and perfect—however, he desires this even more (and is actually able to) because he himself is perfect! It is a beautiful concept to grasp, and if we can live it and experience it, in every area of our lives, I think it could seriously change how we relate to Jesus. Beyond that though, it is vital to know who we are with Christ, before we begin to build these relationships.

Why? If we go in expecting a sub-par gift from God, then that is what we will find. "Seek and you will find." There is a lot of truth to self-fulfilling prophecies, and if you are convinced that because of your sin, or because it has always been this way, or because you are not worthy, or whatever—that you will not be blessed, then most likely you will not find someone who truly blesses you. However, if you understand this principle, God will be able to bless you and lead you into a relationship that is truly good and perfect.

False Belief #2
I Have to Earn God's Love

The second area in which I have seen this faulty understanding manifest is the area of God's love, acceptance, and appreciation. Many Christians feel that either because of their sin, or because of their lack of doing good things, God somehow loves them less than others. Many people feel unworthy of God's love and his acceptance. And many Christians, especially people in the ministry, feel unappreciated for what they do for God, because they never feel they can do enough.

I want to tell you a quick story about my son Samuel. When he was younger, there was a very fun stage when he began to learn how to smile and laugh. So I spent a lot of time doing crazy antics to try and elicit new and funny facial expressions. It was so much fun, and filled me with such joy when he would laugh or smile at me. But sometimes, Samuel was simply done playing. All he wanted was for me to hold him, facing out, so he could watch the environment around him. He loves to watch people walk by—so there would be times where no matter how badly I wanted to play with him, all he wanted was for me to hold him facing out.

So of course I got very angry with him during these times and told him I did not love him anymore because he was not doing anything exciting . . . right? No way! That would be horrible! You see, I love Samuel for who he is not for what he does. This is a huge distinction. He is my son whether he is playing and laughing or staring at a cartoon video! I love him the same! Even (now that he is older) when he disobeys I still love him the same. I would die for him in an instant—no questions asked!

This is the love that God has for you. God says something very interesting in Matthew 3:17—"This is my beloved son, in whom I am well pleased." OK, God is pleased with Jesus because of what he has done right? Because of the incredible ministry and all the healings . . . right? Notice that God says this before Jesus even starts his ministry. This is so different than how so many of us view God—he loved Jesus for who he was—his son. He did not love him because he was so perfect or so miraculous—he loved him because he was his Son. So the lesson here is this—God does not love you, or accept you, or appreciate you more or less based on what you do. He loves you totally and completely because of who you are!

God has unconditional love for you. Conditional love is this—"If you do this, then I will love you." With God, there is no "If—then." It is only, "I love you." No strings attached. Please hear this. Without truly believing this, the church will be ineffective in prayer, evangelism, counseling, and almost everything! We need to begin to live our lives based on a true revelation of God's love, not what this world has taught us about love.

False Belief #3
I Am Not Truly Free From My Sin

The third area in which I see misunderstanding so often is the forgiveness of sins. The Bible promises over and over again with verses like 1 John 1:9:

> If we confess our sins, he is faithful and just and will forgive us our sins and purify us from all unrighteousness.

However, many Christians, both young and old, have a real problem truly living in God's forgiveness. We feel that we must do some sort of good to truly be released. Some even feel that they have incurred God's wrath, and that bad things (like bad relationships, abuse, etc) will begin to happen as punishment for their sins. This is totally against the truth of the gospels. The Bible is painstakingly clear that one Atonement was given for sins, once and for all so that all may be forgiven.

> The death he died, he died to sin once for all (Rom 6:10).

Christ was sacrificed once to take away the sins of many
people...(Hebrews 9:28).

The Bible is also very straight forward concerning the futility of our efforts
to gain righteousness or forgiveness in any way other than simple faith in
Christ.

For it is by grace you have been saved, through faith—and
this not from yourselves, it is the gift of God (Ephesians 2:8).

In other words, it is ridiculous to think that we can add anything to
the work Jesus already did on the cross to free us from sin, and when we beat
ourselves up and refuse to walk in God's total forgiveness we are essentially
trying to do that! Romans 8:1 teaches that there is no condemnation for us,
because Jesus has set us free from the law of death. This is shown perfectly
in the parable of the prodigal son. Although he had sinned in atrocious ways,
his father forgave him with open arms simply because he was his son and he
was repentant.

I am not trying to get too deep here into the theology of atonement.
My main point is this—understanding that you are not a slave but a son or
a daughter frees you to receive into your heart the same forgiveness that
the prodigal son received. And that forgiveness was total and complete and
based solely on sonship.

Please hear my heart in these past few pages. What I am trying to
communicate to you is that before we can discuss what you should look for in
a relationship, we first have to fix the glasses through which you are looking.
That is why I wanted to first lay this foundation of receiving a revelation of
the truth of the Scriptures concerning God's attitude towards his children.
We are not slaves, and therefore we must stop living like we are—under
condemnation, anticipating bad things happening in our lives, not expecting
God to answer our prayers, and not feeling loved or accepted by God.
Instead, we must begin to live like the sons and daughters that God died for
us to become. We must live in his love that is so vast and merciful. We must
live in his acceptance, which is total. We must live in God's promise:

For I know the thoughts I think toward you, says the Lord,
thoughts of peace and not of evil, to give you a future and a
hope (Jeremiah 29:11, NKJV).

When Emotions Become Unrighteous

Begin, then, to set these expectations for yourself in a relationship. I am now going to discuss some problems I have seen in relationships in the emotional realm. Many people are either unaware of these problems or think they will not (or can not) find anything better. This is simply not true when it comes to God's family, and we need to learn to expect good gifts—and this means to be treated well, to be taken care of, and to be happy. I have had a lot of experience in my own life, and with other couples who have been emotionally unrighteous (not whole) because of their pasts, their sin, and/ or their flesh. There are tell-tale signs to watch for that are clearly out of bounds and must be dealt with before a relationship can go any further.

Respecting Each Other's Free Will

Almost all of the emotional difficulties that arise in relationships are rooted in this one sin: one or both of the partners do not respect the other's free will. We need to understand that free will is probably the greatest gift (besides salvation) that God has given to mankind. Free will is what makes us individuals. If we were devoid of free will, we would be computers, robots, or some other matter that is not self-thinking. One of the greatest discoveries a child makes early in their life is the fact that they are an "I." They are not just a "we," but they are distinctive, separate from everyone else, totally unique, independent . . . an "I."

The power to say, "I will do this" or "I will do that"—the power of free will—can be used for immense good or for horrible evils. You see, when God trusted mankind with free will, he did so understanding that he took the risk of us using it for evil. And many of us have. You can think of horrible atrocities where the free will of one man—his God-given ability to make choices independent of the will of God—destroyed many lives. However, free will is also what allows us to truly love. Without free will, "I love you" would be meaningless. But with free will, it is a statement that out of everyone in the world, I use my power of free will to choose you. That spectrum from horrible evils to great goods shows how powerful this gift indeed is.

I say all that to make a point. Knowing that our free wills are gifts from God, and that they are what make us unique, special, and different from everyone else in the world, how can we begin to usurp that from someone else? When we do this we violate a fundamental right of being a human. When we ignore or suppress our loved one's free will we strip them of their identity and their personality. We place them in a box that is only there to please us, and we force them to be something God has not intended them to be. Basically, what we are doing is trying to control this person and force them to do what we want—does that sound like love to you?

In my experience I have seen this kind of sin, not respecting each other's free will, manifest in many ways. What I want to do is describe three different ways I see people act through or with their emotions that are unrighteous and unholy: 1) By putting pressure on each other; 2) By manipulating and controlling each other; and 3) By acting as each other's savior.

What I am hoping you will be able to do is read through these and learn about yourself and your relationship. If you are not in a relationship right now, these are good to know for when you begin to be interested in someone. You can begin to ask yourself questions like "Does this person show traits of this?" I know that I have become so sensitive to manipulation that I can see it in people's words and facial expressions often within minutes of meeting them.

If you are in a relationship I want you to ask yourself—"Do any of these exist in my relationship—or can I foresee any developing later as the commitment is greater?" If you do find that one or more of these are happening in your relationship, then try to figure out who in the relationship is doing it, and lastly, what this tells you about what needs to change in order to have a healthy relationship.

Pressure

It is always wrong for one partner to put pressure on the other partner in order to illicit some outcome that is not necessarily the "other partner's" will or desire. Usually one partner brings pressure because he/she wants the other to do something, or be something in order to fit into their mold for the ideal partner. For instance, in my life I had always assumed that I would marry someone who was an outgoing, vocal leader like myself. So when Mandy and I began to get serious, I noticed that she was not just like me (oh no!).

Without recognizing that I was doing this, I began to subtly push her into leadership roles. I always suggested that she give teachings, even though this made her very uncomfortable. I gave her tons of praise when she did, and acted sorry for myself when she would decide not to. I pressured her into coming to every prayer meeting. I always told her how happy I was that she was a small group leader and asked her if she planned anything new, or wanted to lead other things too. I was always suggesting more, asking for more, subtly insinuating that the more she did in leadership, the happier I would be with her. I used my affection and affirmation to put pressure on her free will.

What I just said might sound nasty and mean to you. But this happens all the time in relationships. One person wants the other person to be something they simply are not. And they are so insecure and afraid of something different than what they think is "right" that they use pressure (sometimes obvious, sometimes not) to try and create their personal utopia. The problem with this, as I have said before, is that you rob your partner of becoming who God has created them to be. Instead, you place yourself as God in their life—and this will only lead to failed relationships and bitterness. A time came in my life where I went through some counseling, and I began to learn how to love. I learned that my job was not to force Mandy to be what I wanted her to be, but to encourage and support her to step out into her dreams—not mine!

Mandy, right now, is not someone who loves the limelight. She does not have to be in front of everyone speaking and leading all the time. She, instead, loves to do the work that no one sees. She loves to find neat little secret ways to bless people. She is always looking out for the person who is left out by the leaders (ironically, since I am a leader, it's usually me leaving them out!). She loves family—she loves to create an environment in our house that is so peaceful and loving that anyone who comes in feels welcomed. I believe there is actually an anointing upon her life to soothe and heal people through simply being warm and loving, and meeting people's needs. She has challenged me so much because I am very different than her in many ways, and I have learned a lot about Jesus' love for people through her. If I had been successful in molding her into my image, I never would have seen this side of her!

This sort of pressure can happen in many ways. There can be pressure to make decisions. One partner may want to go to a certain college and pressure the other to do the same. Or one partner can bring pressure into the relationship when he wants to move and she does not. One insidious form of pressure has to do with marriage. One partner is ready for marriage before the other, and through little comments ("I love that wedding dress, sometimes I wonder if I will ever get to wear one . .") or straightforwardness ("I love you so much—does you not wanting to get married right this very minute mean you don't love me?") puts pressure on the other partner to make the decision to get married before they are ready, just to make their partner happy. Please—if you are reading this and you think—"Hey that sounds like me!"—please understand how serious this is. I know you probably do not want to hear this, but if that is true, your relationship—if you continue—will most likely end in resentment and bitterness. This needs to be dealt with before you go any further.

Pressure can also be put on a partner to do something physical that they simply do not want to do. This is why agreed upon boundaries are so important—if one partner ignores the boundaries, or pushes the limit continually, that should tell you something. Do not listen to the excuse—"I am just so attracted to you!" I have dated, and been engaged, and did not have sex before I was married. I have been in temptation and I know how difficult it can be. But everyone has a choice. And no one is allowed to push you into something you do not want to do. No matter how "attracted" they are to you. That is just an excuse when the truth is—"I do not want to make the effort to restrain myself and stay pure."

There can be pressure to be someone you are not—which I covered earlier when talking about Mandy and I. In a dating relationship both partners should be looking to serve one another, if this is not happening, if your partner is trying to force you to act, feel, or think in ways you do not want to—then they are simply not respecting you or loving you in a Godly way.

Lastly, pressure can be brought through overstatement. One person may say something like "I will love you forever" or "You are everything to me, without you I think I would die." These statements may sound romantic, but are most often exaggerations. When said to someone who loves you, these can put your partner under extreme pressure to reciprocate feelings which in all honesty they may not have, or to make strange promises like, "I will never leave you." It is best to stay away from saying things that push the other person to express a level of affection they may not have yet.

Manipulation and Control

Pressure becomes more insidious when it turns into manipulation and control of the other person. Manipulation differs from pressure in that some negative consequence is threatened if the partner does not acquiesce. What is so sad about this kind of manipulation is that it actually preys on the partner's vulnerability. This is what is so evil about it. One person in the relationship knows that the other loves him, and so he uses that fact to get what he wants by pulling on their emotions, or using his to manipulate the situation.

One way in which this happens that I know a lot about is self-pity. Here is a classic example: When I was dating Mandy, there were times in which we would get into a disagreement. Sometimes during those arguments I would make some hurtful statements that I really did not mean—but they would wound Mandy and she would pull away from me. Mandy is a very loving person and so when I would hurt her, she would take time to think through everything before our actions towards each other would go back to normal again. I am not like that—I am an immediate kind of guy. Once we had solved the problem, I wanted to get on with life as it usually was. In this time of my life, I was also pretty insecure when it came to our relationship—so I wanted to know, quickly, that she still loved me. And how was I going to know this? I needed her to show me some kind of affection.

I am being totally open right now, maybe none of you will ever encounter this—but I think it is a real problem. Instead of talking out the fact that I was insecure, I would instead do things like talk down about myself, or pout, or look visibly upset—anything to get her to give me some attention. You see, that is emotional manipulation—I was using the fact that she loved me, her gift to me, and abusing it to make me feel better about myself. These actions are almost always rooted in insecurity and selfishness. I would use self-pity to get the affection I needed. Have you ever had your partner say something like, "Well I am just the worst girlfriend in the world. I hate myself. I do not know why I am so horrible. . . ." What are you going to say if you love her? Of course something nice, along the lines of—"Oh come on now—you are great! I love you. You are the best girl friend I have ever had . ."

Do you see how this is wrong? It is abusive and controlling. It is using someone else's vulnerability, playing on their emotions, to elicit whatever you need to feel better. Philippians 2:3 says,

> Do nothing out of selfish ambition or vain conceit, but in humility consider others better than yourselves.

This kind of manipulation flies in the face of this verse. Selfish ambition is doing things to make your surroundings more pleasing for you. Vain conceit is being totally full of yourself, and ignorant of others' needs. When we begin to put ourselves first in a relationship in this way, we cease to truly love.

Self-pity is not the only way we manipulate each other emotionally. Anger is a huge tool and is also, unfortunately, one I am familiar with. Anger can be used in many ways to force your partner to give up their free will and do what you want. Imagine a couple where the guy uses anger to force his girlfriend into decisions she is not sure she wants to make. There are times when she wants something to change in the relationship, but because he does not want these changes, he will get angry and yell every time she brings it up. Eventually she will give up, because she does not desire to go through all that yelling and arguing anymore. Some people will also combine that anger with immense affection. I have a friend whose boyfriend, after she broke up with him, went through three cycles of extreme anger and then extreme affection. It sounds ridiculous on paper, but in the real world, you will find many wounded people using these mechanisms to try and keep their lives together.

When anger reaches its climax, of course, you need to watch out for abuse. Anger manifests often through verbal arguments, but it can turn into verbal abuse (calling names, cursing, putting down) and even physical abuse (hitting, slapping, pushing, shoving, grabbing really hard, chasing, etc). For me, these are telltale signs that you need to get out of a relationship. You need to get out, and you need to get help. Especially if there is some sort of physical contact made, you need to get a mature counselor or pastor involved immediately. These are lines that cannot be crossed and show the ultimate loss of respect for another person's free will.

I do not want to bore you with tons of these examples—so I will try to make the rest concise. Guilt trips are used by many people to force their partner into some course of action. We use statements like "I am always trying to do this for you, how come you never do anything?" Or, "If it were me, I would do that for you!" Again, we play on the other person's desire to love us, and use that against them to force them to do our will.

Some other examples are "strings attached actions"—doing things and expecting something in return; holding back affection until you get what you want; giving lots of affection to get what you want; and threatening bad behavior like suicide or drug use or a return to some sin area. These are all ways in which we can control each other, and all are sure signs of a relationship that is becoming unhealthy and needs the intervention of God and the body of Christ.

It is important to remember in the context of this discussion that when these troubles manifest in dating, they will be only more pronounced in marriage. Marriage is like a pressure-cooker, it forces both people to be totally real—and for some people who need to be healed, or freed, that is scary. Some people believe the lie that it will only get better in marriage. Please do not succumb to this—if it is evident already through dating, it is sure only to intensify through engagement into marriage.

Savior Mentality

This is something I did not experience with Mandy, but I actually did do something like this with a girlfriend of mine when I was younger. Basically, when I talk about having a "savior mentality" in dating (or other relationships) I am talking about one person taking care of the other person to an extreme. In every relationship there should be some give and take. And sometimes one person will need to "take" more than the other person. That is natural—but it should balance out with other times when the other person needs to "take" more. It becomes unhealthy when the same person continues to "take" more and more for a long time.

I most often see this happening when one person in the couple has a gift of being "pastoral." People who are like this have a gift from God to take care of people. They often become counselors, nurses, doctors, or caretakers of some kind. This gift, however, can become a snare in a relationship if that person gets together with someone who is needy. Again, much of this is formed in people's pasts. Let's pretend there is a couple named Bob and Wendy. Wendy is raised in a strong Christian family and feels called by God to help people. Her whole life people have always felt comfortable talking to her about their problems. She loves to help people—it makes her feel good about herself to be able to see people get better through what she can offer. (As a side note—Wendy could also be raised in a family where there is a lot of instability, and even as a kid, she tends to be the "peacemaker" in the household). Bob, on the other hand, is raised with a not-so-picture-perfect family. He has especially had trouble ever feeling that his parents loved him. Now, as he enters relationships, he often is looking for someone to affirm him. He wants someone to tell him that they love him, and that he is a great person.

So one day Bob and Wendy meet. They begin to get to know each other, and they are immediately drawn to one another. Why? Is it because of common interests? Obvious relational fit? No. He is drawn to the pastor within her, and she is drawn to the pain inside of him. It's like two magnets pulling on each other. It is so hard to resist. And it is also very hard to see it happening to you. And then—once you are caught, it is also very difficult to get out. Why? Because Wendy won't get out for fear of hurting or crushing Bob—which she can't do since she has to take care of him. And Bob can't get out because he needs Wendy's affection, care, and affirmation.

Why do I call this a "savior mentality"? Essentially, Wendy has become Bob's savior. She has become his need-meeter and not God. There is a balance here. As I said, in every relationship, it is healthy and good to meet each other's needs. It becomes unhealthy, though, when it is unbalanced between the two people. When one person has tons to offer the other, and the other has not much to give back—that is very dangerous. What can happen is that Wendy can so fully meet Bob's needs that his will to follow God is depleted. So while Wendy thinks she is helping him to grow ("I know in a while he will change; be free; be healed; be whole—if I just hold on") she is in fact making him dependent upon her. And this will never lead to healing—only more problems.

So, I write this as a warning, much like the rest of this chapter. Be watchful, be vigilant. Why are you attracted to each other? Is there a healthy give and take, or is it unbalanced? Are you truly "equally yoked"? Because if you are not, you are most likely headed for difficulty in marriage.

Where It Comes From—Have You Been Wounded?

All of these difficulties I have just written about can come from past experiences. How do we learn to have a relationship with someone of the opposite gender? We learn by what we see in our parents. Our parents "model" for us, throughout our entire childhood, what marriage is supposed to look like. Many people in our generation have had "modeling" that has not been good. We have seen separations and divorce at an alarming rate. Many have seen fighting, arguing, cursing, yelling, and screaming. Some have even seen abuse, or been abused. And it is from these experiences that we are now trying to forge our own relationships. No wonder we are having a difficult time!

I challenge you to look closely at what you saw when you were growing up. What messages did you learn about marriage? Did you learn that disagreements are settled through honest discussion or screaming matches? Did you learn that love is shown through only through words, or did actions follow those words? Did you learn that affection is good or bad? Did you learn that mean words can be used whenever and to whomever? Did you learn that if you are not getting your way, you can always just get out?

What I want to draw your attention to is that you did learn something. No matter what your household was like—you learned something. And what you learned has shaped how you treat your girlfriend or boyfriend, and how you will treat your eventual spouse. For many people, you are actually entrenched in a pattern that has come down from generations and you are just about to re-enter it with your own relationship.

How Do You Get Out?

It seems like I am painting a pretty bleak picture here. I am trying to speak so candidly about this, because many people go through life totally ignorant of their own wounds. And as they ignore these hurts and lessons they learned as kids, they continue to reap the "bad fruit" throughout their life.

How can you turn things around? Step number one is getting some objectivity. Objectivity is what we are doing right now—realizing that you might have a problem. Objectivity is looking at yourself, and your relationship, from the outside. It is admitting that you need to change, and need help to do that. This is hard to do. Let's pretend you are in an unhealthy relationship. This will most likely be amazingly hard for you to honestly realize because of your feelings for your partner. The greatest hindrance to being honest with yourself is your fear of hurting the person you love. You would rather continue to lie to yourself about the problems in your relationship, than bring something up and risk hurting your partner—or worse—losing them. Your fear, and your love—both will blind you as you try to be objective. This is why you must often bring in outside opinions. You need some trusted people to see what you cannot see because you are on the inside.

This is the hardest step. Once you can begin to see your own weaknesses, and be honest about the need for you and your relationship to change, then you can begin to move into healing. Often you will need help to overcome these things, especially lessons you have learned over years. So seek out a pastor, counselor, or mentor—and be honest about what you need.

Let me give you an example. I talked earlier of my use of self-pity to manipulate Mandy into showing me affection when we were dating. How did I get out of this? First I needed my pastor-friend (and Mandy) to help me see what I was doing it. Once I saw it, I asked my pastor to do some counseling with me. We discovered where it was coming from in me, and we began the process of healing. The end result, though, had to be change. Mandy would not have just gone ahead with me, simply because I received counseling—she needed to see change. So God has changed me. It wasn't easy, but I chose to not use my emotions to get my way with Mandy. Its funny because Mandy and I became extremely good at recognizing it when each other would do it, and then we would sing the word "manipulation" in a funny way to let the other person know what they were doing. It actually worked very well for us, and we rarely ever do it anymore. God freed us.

So that is my advice—become objective about yourself and your relationship. Be honest, even if it will hurt the other person. It's more important to be true. Then get help. Be humble. Ask God for help. And change.

The Goal

What you are headed for is a relationship in which both people truly have free will. You want a relationship in which neither person is dominating or manipulating. One in which one person is not unequally yoked to the other. By doing this, you will actually make the other person's free will more powerful. By refusing to manipulate each other, and treating each other "right" in God's eyes, you will release each other to truly love back. It is much more powerful for Mandy to show me affection because she wants to, than because I have manipulated it out of her. You should pray to make a relationship atmosphere in which it is safe to express your emotions, thoughts, and feelings without being hurt or disrespected.

I hope you don't struggle with any of this. But for those of you who, when you read this, totally understand what I am talking about, please be careful. Again I re-iterate: If it is happening in dating, it will only be more pronounced in marriage. But there is hope. Be honest with each other, and work on it together. Be willing to lay everything down, including your feelings for each other, to ensure you make the right decision. Marriage is not something to be entered into because you are simply following your woundedness. You want to make this decision in the wholeness and wisdom of God. So seek healing, seek honesty, be unafraid, be true—and God will direct your steps. God will lead you to that "good and perfect gift."

Small Group Discussion Questions:

Christian talks about a girl who said she knew in her head that God loved her, but could not really grasp that with her heart. Can you relate to that? Have you ever felt that way?

In your relationship with God, do you feel more like a slave or like one of his children? Describe how you feel.

Do you ever feel afraid that you will have to "settle" in marriage, not finding someone who really makes you happy? How does that make you feel?

Do you ever struggle with feeling totally forgiven from your past sins? Does this ever make you feel unworthy to receive God's good gifts?

Have you ever been in a relationship (or seen someone else in one) where pressure and/or manipulation and control were exerted to get something out of you? How did that make you feel?

What can you do to avoid getting into relationships with people like that?

Have you ever gotten into a relationship because you wanted to "minister" to them? How did it turn out? Do you think, in general, that is a good idea? Why or why not?

Are there any areas in your life, after reading this chapter, that you think maybe you need healing in before you start dating?

Are the roles of men and women different in dating and marriage?

Learning to submit to one another in love

I have a friend who recently went out on a date. She had met someone at a Christian function. They hit it off, and decided to get together for coffee and a talk. She was pretty excited about it and went into the conversation with much anticipation. However, somewhere between ordering the coffee and finishing it, things went terribly wrong.

While discussing some common friends of theirs who had recently been married, her date said something to the effect of, "I think they are great for each other, I just hope she can learn to submit to him better." My friend was a little taken back, "What do you mean?" "Well," he responded, "You know that men are the head of the household and women are meant to be subservient." As she opened her mouth to begin some healthy debate on this topic, he pointed his finger at her and exclaimed, "You be quiet! Women should learn in quietness and submission!" Apparently not only did wives have to submit to husbands, but in his view women in general were second-class to men.

Are you wondering where this guy got his ideas? He would tell you, very strongly I presume from the conversation, that his ideas come straight from the Bible—don't you read it?

Let me tell you one more story. I was driving some soccer players in my car several years ago. I mentioned something about a woman I knew in leadership and one of them made a degrading comment (these were Christian boys) about women being unable to lead. I challenged him and asked him why he thought that. He went on to tell me that no woman could ever lead as well as a man—even in the secular realm! God has just created them inferior. They are too emotional. They really should never be leaders— that's up to men.

I challenged him to find that in the Bible before our next soccer practice. He came to me the next day with a couple references (all unfortunately out of context and having nothing to do with women in secular leadership). The most amazing part of this story, however, did not come from the boy. (Brace yourself). As we were talking, a voice lifted above the noise of soccer practice yelling out my name. It was his dad, calling to me from his car. "Coach Dunn, read your Bible, it's in there!"

It Matters for Dating

I have spent the past several chapters giving advice about dating. We have discussed learning more about each other and ourselves, how to remain holy, and how to follow God. We have also looked at some telltale signs of things going wrong in a relationship. The rest of the book will look at good signs for relationships going in the right direction, but before we move into that, I need to address this very important topic.

Roles of men and women in a marriage are established long before "I do." It is crucial to know what you are getting into in this area. It will determine how you make decisions as a couple, how you raise your children, how you relate to each other, what kind of church you attend together, and more. I find, though, that not many couples talk about this extensively. Therefore, I want to devote some time specifically to this topic. But I do not just want to contend that it should be talked about—that is clear. I want to offer a view of our roles in marriage that many of you may never have had the chance to hear about. And yes—it is in your Bible!

In talking to teens and young adults about this topic, I have realized that many young Christians who are beginning to date and look for a life partner are not sure what they believe about godly roles in marriage. Many people by default begin to adhere to the "man is the leader, woman is subservient" model. I can say with much confidence that the Bible does not lay out any set standards like this for marriage across the board. It does not anywhere tell men to lead their household, or to be the "priest of the home" (Groothuis, 150) as I have heard some say.

This is why I must write this chapter. But I have to make a disclaimer. This topic is astronomically huge in the church, and has been for years. It is incredible how much literature has been written on this topic alone. There are entire books written on just one piece of a certain text and whole articles written on just one Greek word. Most of these are written by people much more educated than I am.

So what I am going to attempt to do in this chapter will not give you a thorough explanation of anything on this topic. I am not an authority on this topic. All I am is a small-town pastor who has read some about this, and truly feels in his heart and head that many people are misinterpreting the Scriptures in their conclusions on this topic. So I am going to give you an overview of what I believe the Bible says. I will also be citing various works that support many of the points I will be making—mostly to show you that I am not alone at all in my views. I will not be able to deal with every nuance, or maybe even every Scripture that relates, but I just want to try to give you a different feel for this topic. I want to make you think. I want to challenge your pre-conceived notions, and make you re-read your Bible a little.

Old Glasses—Our Biases

I have very good eyesight, so I have never in my life needed glasses. My parents, on the other hand, are blind as bats. As a kid I sometimes thought it was fun to put on my dad's glasses and walk around and see what it was like. I never understood why he would wear those, because when I put them on everything around me looked weird—cabinets looked taller, furniture looked slightly circular, and everything far away was blurry—the truth was being distorted because I was wearing the wrong glasses.

I believe it is true that sometimes what we think about the Bible is based on the "glasses" we read it through. Our glasses consist of our biases and pre-conceived ideas. For instance, many of us have it ingrained in our heads that men are the head of the household and that women are to be servants long before we ever truly study what the Bible actually teaches. This is just the way it is. And for anyone to threaten that viewpoint makes us very uncomfortable. But I want to challenge you to consider that maybe the glasses you are wearing are wrong. What if they are distorting the truth?

I want to give you this "glasses" analogy because I fear that you might skim over this chapter and not give it much credence because you have already made up your mind. I know, I used to believe exactly like you do. But as I began to read the Scriptures with a different understanding, they began to make much more sense to me. So please, take a second to re-read this with me, and see what you think. Take off your old glasses for a second.

Proof-Texting—The Danger of Overstating a Situational Verse
What if you walked into church and your pastor was preaching that Christians were not allowed to drink only water, but they had to (Biblically) include other beverages in their diet? I have some friends who drink only water for health reasons; do they know that the Bible says not to do that? Also—when was the last time you drank some wine? What if your pastor began to teach that you were in sin if you did not drink wine on a regular basis?

I'm sure you know where I am going with this—1 Timothy 5:23 reads, "Stop drinking only water, and use a little wine . ." There it is. The Bible clearly tells you that it is wrong to drink only water, and you must drink wine on occasion. What? You disagree? Good. Why is what I am saying here wrong? It is because Paul is obviously writing this only to Timothy, right? That is what we would call a cultural truth of the Bible, and not a transcendent one. Cultural truths in the Bible are ones meant for a specific time and a specific person or church, but were not meant to be applied universally across time, culture, and people. Transcendent truths were applicable in the current cultural setting of the Bible, as well as in every time and culture to follow.

To make things more confusing, some verses taken literally are only meant for the culture they were written in, but the principle behind the verse is meant universally. Take for example Galatians 5:2—"Mark my words! I, Paul, tell you that if you let yourselves be circumcised, Christ will be of no value to you at all." Is Paul saying here that if a man today is physically circumcised, that Christ will be of no value to him? If that were true, that would mean that the majority of men in America would not be able to avail themselves of Christ's work on the cross!

Of course you know that is not the correct way to view this verse. This verse was written to a specific people, in a specific time, for a specific situation. Paul was writing here in his letter to the Galatians to rebuff the "Judaizers" who wanted to make Christians adhere to the Jewish law. He was saying that the Jewish law could not save them—only Christ could. And that is precisely the meaning of 5:2. It could be stated, "If you rely on the law for salvation, than Christ will be of no value to you." Does that make sense? He did not want the Greek Christians to be forced to observe the Jewish law by being circumcised. He wanted them to be saved by grace, not by works.

So what do we do with this verse? Clearly we cannot argue that it is a universal truth that being circumcised will disqualify you from Christ's grace. That was a cultural truth. But there is a transcendent principle in this verse that does apply across time and culture. This principle is restated in Ephesians 2:9, "For it is by grace you have been saved . . not by works, so that no one can boast." The transcendent truth is that we cannot save ourselves by taking action (living holy, going to church, doing good deeds), but that salvation is only by God's grace.

When people take verses and apply them incorrectly, that is called taking it "out of context." What is the context? Well you need to look at why the author was writing this, who he was writing it to, what culture did they live in (Jewish, Greek, or Roman), as well as the overall themes and feeling of the letter, and other verses in the Bible (just as we did in the previous paragraph with Ephesians 2:9). Please keep this in mind as we continue our discussion. There are verses like Ephesians 5:22, "Wives, submit to your husbands as to the Lord" that, taken out of context, have hurt people for years. So what does this verse actually say? We need to understand what was meant just for the culture and time in which it was written, and what was meant to universally apply to us.

Creation—Men And Women Created in Equality For Partnership

If we want to discuss God's will for the relationship between men and women, especially in marriage, it makes sense to look to the beginning. In the Creation accounts in Genesis we find some very powerful explanations of God's will for men and women. The Bible describes for us God's original intentions for how men and women should relate as husbands and wives. We also find an example, so early in the Bible, of what we just talked about: One verse, being taken out of context and used to oppress women for years.

To prove my point more strongly I am going to borrow some material from a teaching one of my pastors, Rev. Lynn Latshaw, has given several times. Before discussing specific passages, I want to focus on one very important Hebrew word—*ezer*. Now I am not going to tell you what this word means yet, but I want to instead look at how it is used in other contexts to decipher its meaning (a method often used to find meanings of words in the Bible).

Here are several scriptures where this word is used in the Bible.

Read over them and take a second to come up with some words that could fit in the place of *ezer*.

> Hear, O Lord, and be merciful to me; O Lord, be my *ezer*
> (Psalm 30:10).

> We wait in hope for the Lord; He is our *ezer* and our shield
> (Psalm 33:20).

> Yet I am poor and needy; Come quickly to me, O God. You
> are my *ezer* and my deliverer; O Lord, do not delay
> (Psalm 70:5).

So what does this word mean? Can you make some guesses from the context? From classes I have been in where Lynn has done this, some words people have suggested are: strength, defense, defender, stronghold, fortress, etc.

You may have already guessed where I am going with this, but let me show you one more verse where *ezer* is used:

> The LORD God said, "It is not good for the man to be alone.
> I will make a(n) *ezer* suitable for him"
> (Genesis 2:18).

How is that word translated in your Bible? It is translated as "helper" in the NIV and NKJV. When you hear the word "helper," does it carry the same meaning as what *ezer* means by looking at the verses above? When we think of helper we think of someone who is subservient and inferior. In the ministry I used to lead, we had several interns. These interns in many ways were my "helpers." They were of lower "rank" than me, and they basically did what I asked them to do. That is what we think when we read this verse—but it is not at all what the Hebrew is saying.

The word *ezer* is used 21 times in the OT. 18 of those are used to refer to God, and 17 describe him as the "helper of Israel." When you think of God as being our "helper" do you think he is inferior and subservient to us? No way!

The point I am making here is that our understanding of this verse must change. Why is this such a big deal? It's a big deal because many people begin their thinking about the roles of men and women in marriage with this verse. They will argue that women were created inferior to men, created to serve men, or created to help men, but not be in full equal partnership with men. This is so powerfully damaging to women in marriage—and it is not even true! This was never God's intention in this verse. The Holy Spirit could have used a different Hebrew word if He had wanted to describe women as subservient and inferior to their husbands, but he chose not to. He chose to use ezer. Why? Because he intended for men and women to function together in equal partnership. Just look at these verses in Genesis 1:26-27:

> Then God said, "Let us make human beings in our image, in our likeness, so that *they may rule . . .*" So God created human beings in his own image, in the image of God he created them; *male and female he created them* (emphasis mine).

At one point in my life I had never read these verses with "unbiased glasses." I always assumed that God made man in his image, and woman in the image of man, not God. I always assumed that man was given authority to rule and have dominion and that women were given to help the man do this. But I have discovered that my assumptions were simply unbiblical. The Bible states that men and women together were created in God's image, and they were together, as a team or partnership, given authority to rule. That is the beginning of what was a paradigm shift for me.

From all this, I am hoping that you can begin to see that maybe, just maybe, the whole idea of women being second class in marriage could be non-biblical. If we read Genesis understanding what the author intended it to mean, rather than ascribing incorrect meaning to an English translation, I think we have to face the fact that God did not create women to be inferior. He created her to be a partner and a co-laborer with the man. In Genesis 1:28 God actually commands them both to be fruitful and to rule the earth. Both of them together! He didn't just command Adam—he commanded them to do it as a team. That is so powerful!

The only time that anything is said about the woman being subservient is after they have sinned and God is telling them the consequences of their sins. He said in Genesis 3:16, "Your desire will be for your husband, and he will rule over you." Clearly, if this was God's intended will, he would not have made it a repercussion of sin. The very fact that it is listed as a result of sin shows that it is not what God intended for marital relationships!

Some will still argue, though, that since then, we are still under the "Fall" and therefore women should be ruled by their husbands. I believe, however, that the whole message of the New Testament refutes that argument. When Jesus died and rose again, he freed us from bondage to sin! Right? So why live under that curse, if Jesus has set us free? Why force women to live under the repercussions of sin, when Jesus died to free us from the results of sin? That's why he came! There are so many verses I could quote to support my point here. Here is one:

> Christ redeemed us from the curse of the law [the curse
> is the consequence of not fully keeping the law—in other
> words, sin] by becoming a curse for us (Galatians 3:13).

So why, if Christ has redeemed us from the curse, should we force women to continue under it? In conclusion, from Genesis we do not see women being created to be second in command, or assistants, or helpers. Rather, we see them called by God and intended by God to be man's partner and companion—to rule and have dominion together.

The Culture of the Day—A Key to Understanding Scriptures on Marriage

Now that we have some understanding that God did not intend from Creation for women to be lesser than men, but for them to be partners, we can turn our attention to the culture in which the New Testament was written. Why is it important to look at the culture? It is important because it gives us an understanding of how people of their time would understand what the writers of the Bible were saying.

For instance, does the following sentence make sense to you? "Sunday Night starts at 7:00 at the barn." What does that statement mean to you? Am I asserting that nighttime on Sundays starts at 7:00pm? How about 7:00am? Or am I saying that only in barns does nighttime start at 7:00, but in other places of the world, it's different? Maybe you can infer (even though I don't say it) that I am referring to a meeting—even then, does this make much sense to you? Where do we meet, in a barn? Are there horses there? Hay? Stalls? What kind of meeting is Sunday Night?

This is a statement from the announcements of our church. You cannot understand it fully because you are not part of our "church culture" since you do not attend our church. Let me tell you some about our "culture." People who attend our church refer to our building affectionately as "the barn." It was renovated 25 years ago, and certainly only looks similar to a barn on the outside. "Sunday Night" is the name of our youth meeting on, you guessed it, Sunday nights. People only know the "code words" we use in our culture if they are familiar with our culture. In the same way cultures of old had their own understandings of marriages, male and female roles, and submission. The writers of the Bible were "of" that culture, so they knew how to write to that culture. However, when we read the Bible, we struggle sometimes with interpretation because we are not of that culture.

So that is why it makes sense to at least get a general idea about the three major cultures that co-existed in the time that most of the New Testament was written. As you probably know from reading the account of Jesus' birth, the Roman Empire ruled the land in which all of the NT occurrences take place. Within the Roman Empire, there was a division. The Western part of the empire was more fully Roman than the eastern part. What I mean is the cities in the western part of Roman rule had more fully adopted Rome's ideals, beliefs, and ways of life. The eastern section of the Roman empire, while still submitted to Roman law and rule, took much of its cultural norms from its rich Ancient Greek heritage (Payton, 13). Therefore the culture known as Greco-Roman or Hellenistic emerged. And thirdly, of course, is the Jewish culture. As we see clearly by reading the Gospels, the Jewish culture had a very distinct and separate culture from both Roman and Hellenistic cultures. They even had their own laws and courts (the Sanhedrin). So it is within this cultural milieu that the Bible was written.

It is important to gain an understanding of these cultures, as I stated earlier, because the authors of the NT understood as they were writing the Scriptures how best to communicate to the cultures to which they were writing. Now, it would be too exhaustive for this chapter to look in depth into all the distinctions of these three cultures, so we will briefly examine only their beliefs on women, since that is obviously pertinent to this chapter and book.

Jewish Culture

Let's begin briefly with the Jewish culture of the day. An interesting place to start is a prayer from early Judaism (before the time of the NT) that was repeated often by men throughout the Jewish culture:

> A man must recite three benedictions every day: 'Praised
> [be Thou, O Lord . . .] who did not make me a gentile . . . a
> boor [ignoramus] . . . [or] a woman.' (Keener, 161)

In his book, *Paul, Women, and Wives*, Keener goes on to talk of a teacher with whom Paul would be familiar. This teacher "advised men not to sit among women, because evil comes from them like a moth emerging from clothes. A man's evil, this teacher went on to complain, is better than a woman's good, for she brings only shame and reproach" (161). Many writers in Jewish culture thought of women as "unstable and overly talkative" (163) while others thought that even God avoided talking to women in order to steer clear of any perceived unholiness He might have simply from associating with them (162)!

Another writer, a philosopher named Philo, describes the wife's proper duty as "slave service." While Josephus, a well-known historian of that time, has this to say:

> The woman, says the Law, is in all things inferior to the man.
> Let her accordingly be submissive, not for her humiliation,
> but that she may be directed; for the authority has been
> given to the man (165).

Most Jewish writers shared this view, and reflect the cultural norm that to be a "good" wife was to be submissive and obedient—even to the point of slave-like servanthood (166).

Hellenistic Culture

By the time Rome had come into power, the culture of Ancient Greece had been in place for three centuries. This culture is the one that defined what is now referred to as the Hellenistic culture (Payton, 13). In Ancient Greece, women had almost no legal rights. They could not buy or sell property, or engage in business. They also were not allowed to appear in public without a man. The only women who did appear in public without a man were prostitutes. Because of this, it was considered wrong for a woman to talk to a man other than her husband. There was an interesting exception in this culture though—a group of women called the hetairai. These were women who had received an education in mainland Greece, and, returned, now able to discuss and debate with the men. This group of women became known as the hetairai because they were intellectually fulfilling for men, but as their role evolved, they also began to do sexual acts with these men—beginning another form of prostitution. The way people knew if a woman was a hetairai was if she spoke openly with men in public (Payton, 14).

In summary then, women were not allowed to speak to men in

public, other than their husbands. If they did, it would ruin their reputation, as well as that of the men who talked with them. The only women who did speak openly in public with men were the hetairai—high-class prostitutes (Payton, 14).

Roman Culture

Out of the three cultures, the Roman culture was the most favorable towards women. Women were not viewed as the property of their husbands (as they were in the other two cultures). They could own property, manage finances, even divorce their husbands. They could also speak publicly with men without ruining their reputation (Payton, 13). However, even with that being true, there are signs in the literature of the day that the men in the upper class of Roman culture were beginning to feel threatened by these new found freedoms of women (Keener, 144).

There is evidence that in fact there was increasing anti-feminist writing and satire at the time. A sign that a longing for male dominance was emerging—a backlash against the freedoms of these women (Keener, 145). The upper class had an ideal of "a 'benevolent patriarch,' who ruled fairly on behalf of those under him, but maintained his own superior rank and social status" (Keener, 143). This was, in fact, so important that the Roman Senate actually passed laws to ensure that in the wake of women gaining rights, the male dominance in the family would not be lost (Keener, 144).

An Evangelistic Message

Why is all this information important? Many articles I have read argue that we have to look at the writings of the New Testament in context—not just the context of the chapters around it, but also the historical context (Payton, 13). When we read the Bible, we must understand that not all verses (as I began this chapter by explaining) are meant to be transcendent truth—that is, applying to all Christians for all time. In fact some were meant very specifically for people in the city (Ephesus for instance) that the writer was addressing.

Therefore, knowing the culture to which the writers were writing sheds light on why they have said some of what they said. For instance—the major apparent "injunctions" against women in marriage are found in 1 Timothy, 1 Corinthians, 1 Peter, and Ephesians, letters written to churches in specific cities or regions. It is interesting to note that all of these cities (Ephesus for Timothy and Ephesians; Corinth for Corinthians; and five cities in Asia Minor for Peter) are located in the Eastern part of the Roman Empire, landing them in the middle of the Hellenistic culture. So it makes a lot of sense for us to know how poorly women were viewed in this culture, and the many rules taking away their rights, including talking with men.

Keener argues that Paul was attempting to make the church as evangelistic as possible. His goal was to reach as many people as he could with the Gospel. In fact, in 1 Corinthians 9:22 he states, "I have become all things to all men so that by all possible means I might save some." Keener says "Paul portrayed Christian ethics in terms that would best communicate to their culture the moral superiority of Christianity." He "understood the particular values of ancient society well enough to know how best to impact it" (157). In other words, without watering down the gospel at all, he made sure that he communicated the values and principles of Christianity in a way that didn't purposefully alienate the culture he was trying to reach.

So it makes sense that he would write something like "women should remain silent in the churches . . . if they want to inquire about something, they should ask their own husbands at home" (1 Cor. 14:34-35). Why does this make sense? Because if Paul allowed women in that church to speak openly with men, what would new comers and non-believers think? They would think that Christianity allowed prostitutes like the hetairai to have authority in the church to speak! Paul elsewhere tells women to pray and prophesy out-loud in meetings (1 Cor. 11:5) so obviously he is not saying this can't happen anywhere. He is instructing the church to be in tune with the culture and to not do anything they knew would hurt their witness. Sometimes for the sake of the gospel, Christians even have to restrict their own freedoms in Christ.

For instance, I once heard a story of Christian and Muslim missionaries who went to China to draw people to their faiths. The Christians refused to learn the Chinese language, culture, or traditions—and simply did their services the way they did them in the West. The Muslims however, took time to study the Chinese culture and even learn the language. And they won thousands to their faith. They were willing to restrict their freedom to better communicate their faith, and it was highly effective. This is exactly what Paul is telling the Corinthians to do. Doesn't this make sense?

So when we read some of the difficult passages in the Bible, we must understand that the writers were writing to a different time and a different culture than the one we live in today in America. We must take that into account, or else we are in danger of misinterpreting the Scriptures and using them incorrectly.

The Scripture

With that foundation now laid, let's now look at the verses that seem to cause people to believe that women are to be subservient to men in marriage. Where do we get this idea? And is that truly what the author and God intended when these verses were written? You will see that in fact the opposite is true. Nowhere in the Bible does it actually tell men to take authority over their wives (Groothuis, 150; Keener, 18). People have inferred this conclusion from Scriptures that are difficult to understand, and created doctrines of men that are not God's doctrines.

Submission in the Face of Adversity (1 Peter 3:1)

Let's start in Peter, because most people are in unity about what this passage is referring to. Peter, starting in 1 Peter 2:18, begins to talk about submission. He begins with slaves, then moves to wives, and then to husbands. A major focus of his submission is the need for Christians, sometimes, to submit to conditions that are not favorable—as Christ did. He says this to slaves in verses 18-19:

> Slaves, submit yourselves to your masters with all respect,
> not only to those who are good and considerate, but also to
> those who are harsh. For it is commendable if a man bears
> up under the pain of unjust suffering because he is conscious
> of God.

Peter goes on to say, "to this you were called, because Christ suffered for you." In the following verses he tells of all the unjust ways that Christ suffered—when he certainly did not deserve to. And yet he did not fight back because he knew he was doing it for God.

Then, in 3:1 Peter begins, "Wives, *in the same way* be submissive to your husbands" (emphasis mine). This "in the same way" is referring to this same submissiveness Jesus displayed in the face of adversity (Groothuis, 173). The most telling part of this passage is after he says for wives to be submissive to their husbands. It reads, "so that, if any of them do not believe the word, they may be won over without words by the behavior of their wives..." However, the "if any" part of that verse is disputed. Belleville argues that the Greek wording for this verse does not imply a hypothetical situation (i.e.—"if perhaps someone is married to an unsaved person") but indeed is making a statement of fact (119). In other words, Peter was addressing a specific problem that existed then. Belleville states that a better translation would read, "So that even though some of them have rejected the Word..."(119).

Therefore, we know that Peter is writing to a real situation that is happening—Christian women in the young Christian churches are married to unbelievers. Is Peter, then, actually telling wives to submit to the spiritual leadership of a non-Christian? The kind of "submission" that you hear talked about in churches today—is that what he is advocating? I don't think that is plausible. One author describes the problem by saying that in that culture it would be easy for a man to change religions (become a Christian) even if his wife didn't. The reason is that in their culture the husband had ruling authority over this wife, and therefore could force her to attend whatever religion he chose. If a woman got saved though, and the husband did not—that was trouble. She could not push her views on him, because in their culture she was less than him (Groothuis, 173). So Peter tells the woman to be submissive in the face of adversity—just as he has been saying all throughout the preceding passages. Therefore it can be clearly seen that this one verse "be submissive to our husbands" is not a rule to be established across time that women are to be ruled by their husbands, or that husbands are to "spiritually lead" their wives. In fact it does not say either of those in this passage. We are forced to not take this out of context. A major reason for this passage, then, is to encourage wives to be submissive in those circumstances, so as to imitate Christ and hopefully win their husband over—"in the same way" as Jesus did.

Another major reason for this passage is to encourage mutual submission in marriage. Verse 7 begins "Husbands, in the same way . ." reiterating the fact that this was expected of both husbands and wives (Bilezikian, 189). As we will see with other texts, Peter is asserting the mutual submission of wives to husbands, husbands to wives, and all Christians to all Christians. He ends telling the husbands that their wives are "heirs with you of the gracious gift of life." And that if the husband does not recognize that, his prayers could be hindered (vs. 7)!

Lastly, I want to emphasize two points about this verse. First, do you see how many people just take part of that verse—"be submissive to your husbands"—and run with it, without realizing the full context of the verse? Do you see the danger in that? And second, this verse is also important for what it does not say. Notice that it does not say anything like "Husbands take authority over your wives" or "Wives, you are second class in marriage and must obey your husband." Submission and obedience are vastly different, a point we will cover in depth soon.

Redefining Headship (Ephesians 5:23 and 1 Corinthians 11:3)

Just looking at one passage, we can already see the role that culture and context play in interpreting the Scripture. Another major area of debate surrounds the term "headship." There are two Scriptures that use the term "head" (Gk—kephale) to refer to relationships. In Ephesians 5:23 Paul writes that the "husband is the head of the wife as Christ is the head of the church," and in 1 Corinthians 11:3 he states that "the head of the woman is man."

Many people have taken these Scriptures to mean that by creation man is over woman. When you hear the word "head" what do you think? In our culture we often think about a CEO or a President—someone in charge. However, as we have already discussed from Genesis, God did not create women to be inferior or subservient to men, so what does "head" mean if not "master?"

The word kephale is used by Paul 18 times. This word is translated in three different ways depending on its context—(1) source or beginning, (2) leader or ruler, (3) prominent or preeminent (Belleville, 123). It is difficult to make a sweeping translation; therefore Paul's passages must be taken one at a time. Below are three scriptures in which "head" is meant similarly.

> And he is the head of the body, the church; he is the
> beginning and the firstborn from among the dead, so that in
> everything he might have supremacy (Colossians 1:18).

> He has lost connection with the Head, from whom the
> whole body, supported and held together by its ligaments
> and sinews, grows as God causes it to grow (Colossians 2:19).

> We will in all things grow up into him who is the Head,
> that is, Christ. From him the whole body, joined and held
> together by every supporting ligament, grows and builds
> itself up in love (Ephesians 4:15).

These three passages clearly point to an understanding of the word "head" that is consistent with the "origin," "source," or "beginning" translation (Belleville, 123). The text asserts that he is the "beginning" and the "firstborn." It also says that the whole body is caused to grow from its connection with the head. In other words he is the "source of cohesion" (Belleville, 124) of the whole body, and the source from which the body is to get its life to grow. Now let's look at two other Scriptures:

> You have been given fullness in Christ, who is the head over
> every power and authority (Colossians 2:10).

> ...far above all rule and authority, power and dominion, and
> every title that can be given . . . And God placed all things
> under His feet and appointed him to be head over everything
> for the church, which is His body, and the fullness of Him
> who fills everything in every way (Ephesians 1:22).

In these two passages, based on the context—"under His feet" and "far above all"—it can be seen that these two uses of the word head more clearly mean "preeminent" or "supremacy" (Belleville, 124). It is highly doubtful that he is saying Christ is the source or the leader of every power, including demonic powers.

Once we understand the fact that this word has varied meanings, then based on the context we can more accurately look at the verses concerning women and men. The two verses I want to examine are Ephesians 5:23 and 1 Corinthians 11:3. Both have been understood by some to indicate the rulership of a husband over his wife, however in light of our understanding of the different meanings of the word "head" it becomes evident that an alternate understanding is more correct.

In Ephesians 5:23, after Paul says that the husband is the head of the wife, he then says "as Christ is the head of the church, his body." Based on the context of this verse, it is clear that the meaning of the word head is not the contemporary idea of Head as a CEO, or Lord, or even the idea of supremacy or preeminence. Rather the meaning is the idea of origin or source (Belleville, 124-6); that is, Jesus is the origin or source of the life and growth of the church.

Understanding this idea begins to change our concept of "head." Mandy and I still believe that I am the "head" of my wife—but that does not mean that I am the master, in charge, or have the final say. It means that in some way—"a profound mystery" as Paul says a couple verses later in Ephesians—I am the source or origin for our marriage. I also believe this is referring to the simple fact that Adam was created chronologically before Eve, and that Eve was created from Adam's rib—thus making man the source or origin of women. Nowhere does this verse, or any other, say that women are to be considered man's slaves or less than men in any way. The

Corinthians verse sheds even more light.

> Now I want you to realize that the head of every man is
> Christ, and the head of the woman is man, and the head of
> Christ is God (1 Corinthians 11:3).

This verse begins one of the most confusing texts in the Bible—a passage
full of cultural nuances that even our best scholars grapple with for
understanding. Many try to make this verse mean that not only in marriage,
but also in all areas of society, culture, life, etc men are superior to women.
It is so unfortunate that people can distort God's words like that.

I cannot go into all the intricacies of this text, but as I have been
trying to do throughout this chapter, I want to offer you a brief explanation
to challenge how you have looked at this verse in the past, and hopefully spur
you on to dig deeper into the true meaning, rather than simply accepting our
culture's interpretation. As I said, many read this text and oppress women
with it, but if you read a little further you are confronted with some startling
verses in 1 Corinthians 11:11-12:

> In the Lord [These three words are an important
> introduction. Paul is making the assertion that some things
> may be true for the culture we are in, but as Christians
> something else is true], however, woman is not independent
> of man, *nor is man independent of woman* (italics added). For
> as woman came from man, so also man is born of woman.
> But everything comes from God.

Clearly Paul is making a statement here similar to Galatians 3:28 where
he emphatically goes against the culture and declares, "There is neither . .
male nor female, for you are all one in Christ Jesus." Does Paul say this in
Galatians, and then declare in Corinthians that women are inferior? He does
not.

Again there are many ways to view 1 Corinthians 11:3. I want
to challenge you though—rather than view it as a chain of command or
hierarchy (Groothuis, 150) look at it as a chronological order. An order of
who came from what. This is again taking "head" to mean origin or source.
Read it that way and it makes complete sense—man came from Christ
because Christ created man; woman came from man because God used man's
rib from which to form her; and Christ came from God as the Son of God

incarnate (Groothuis, 159).

    This actually makes more sense than viewing it the other way. Why? Well let's think about it. If it was a list of who is in charge of whom, shouldn't it read, "God the head of Christ, Christ the head of man, man the head of woman?" That would be the "right" order according to many, but instead it is different. If you look at it from the origin perspective though, the order makes total sense. Christ made man first (John 1:3, Col 1:16), then woman was made from man (Genesis 2:21-22), and last Christ came to earth from the Father (John 1:1, 14; 8:14, 42) (Groothuis, 159).

    OK, so have I bored you with technicalities yet? I know, I know—Greek words, culture this and culture that, picking apart verses, listening to different arguments—it can all become wearisome. Is the Bible that difficult to interpret? At times it is, but only if you want to get to the truth. But to me, while complicated by humans like myself, it feels simple in my heart. It makes sense to me in my mind too. I am not afraid to say that Scripture asserts the headship of man in marriage; I just have a different idea of headship. I do not believe that the Scripture creates a "position" for husbands as the CEO, leader, President, or priest of the home. That simply is not in Scripture. Just because we think "head" means that in English, does not mean that's what it meant when Paul used that word. And I am convinced that in fact Paul intended for us to understand the spiritual position of the husband being the source or origin of the wife. I have heard it described by my pastor as "headwaters." So whatever flows out of the husband—be it holy living, prayer, or even sin—will flow into the spiritual lives of his wife and children. With that view it becomes an awesome responsibility, and not a power trip.

Mutual Submission

The last major idea pulled from Scripture about women and men in marriage that I want to tackle is the whole idea of "submission." As I will show briefly, there is no question that wives are called to submit to their husbands. However, there are two problems with our common understanding of that sentence. First, when we think of "submission," we think "obedience," and this is an incorrect translation of that word. Second, when we assert this over wives, we ignore the same exact command from Scripture for men to submit to their wives.

    Below I have listed four texts that people often quote to assert the need for women to submit to their husbands.

Wives, submit to your husbands as to the Lord
(Ephesians 5:22).

Wives, submit to your husbands, as is fitting in the Lord
(Colossians 3:18).

Train the younger women . . . to be subject to their husbands
(Titus 2:4-5).

Wives, in the same way, be submissive to your husbands
(1 Peter 3:1).

Note that in none of these passages does the term "obey" appear. There is
a major difference between being told to be submissive and being told to
obey (Belleville, 188; Keener, 156) "Obedience is something demanded of
someone in a lesser position" (Belleville, 118), thus slaves (Eph 6:5; Col 3:22)
and children (Eph 6:1; Col 3:20) are told to obey those in authority over them.
Therefore it is very telling that Paul chose not to use the word "obey" when
addressing wives in the same exact passages! Obviously, we must interpret
this to mean that he did not mean for wives to "obey" their husbands, but to
submit—which, again, is different.

So if submission does not mean obedience, as is often how popular
Christianity has defined it, what does it mean? Submission, in this context,
is one person's decision to serve another—not because they are lesser—but
rather as an equal deciding to serve another equal. "Submission...is a
voluntary act of deferring to the wishes of an equal" (Belleville, 118). Further
confirmation of this point is found by looking at the Greek word used for
submission. An accurate look at the way in which the word is written lets us
know the meaning is more like "to place oneself under" than it is "to be ruled
by an authority greater than oneself" (Belleville, 118).

Do you see the major difference in this? I know I have been quoting
a lot of books here, but let me talk to you in my own voice for a second.
Basically, in the same way we have misunderstood the meaning of headship—
thinking it meant CEO when actually it means "source" in the context—we
have misunderstood the meaning of submission. We have thought it to mean
obedience of a lesser person to the ruling person in marriage, when in reality
all that it means is for one equal to serve and lay down their life for another
equal. Still not convinced? Still think that men are called to be the spiritual
leader of the house, the priest of the home, the ruler, CEO, and boss? Have

you read Ephesians 5:21, the verse before the verse that tells women to submit to their husbands?

This is one of the most overlooked truths in the Bible. Verse 21 says this: "Submit to one another out of reverence for Christ." The very next verse says, "Wives submit . . ." and then four verses later says, "Husbands, love your wives…" It is all one thought (Belleville, 118). In fact the Greek word for submission does not even appear in verse 22 (Keener, 169). "It is clear that the submission of verse 22 [wives] cannot be other than the submission of verse 21 [all Christians]" (Keener, 169). Verse 22, therefore could be translated, "For example, wives submit to your husbands" (Keener, 169).

I know I have used a lot of books here. Let me distill it for you again. Basically many people take those two verses and try to separate them. In fact (look in your Bible) they often put a subheading between those verses so it is even harder to know they should go together. If you took Verse 22 about women submitting to husbands alone—in the Greek it would not even say submit. It pulls its meaning from the previous verse. Without the previous verse it would have no meaning. This is telling because the previous verse tells us all to submit to one another. Wives submitting to husbands is just one example of Christian submission to one another. Therefore, wives should submit because all Christians should submit (Keener, 169). We are all called to submit to each other—male to female and female to male—we are all one in the Lord (Gal 3:28). Paul then goes on to give specific instructions as to how each person can do that! Wives do this . . .Husbands do this . . . Do you see it?

Picture it this way. A couple comes to me for marriage counseling. Let's say their names are Mary and John. After a long session of all their complaints I say to them, "You need to submit to each other, you need to serve each other. Mary, submit to John by respecting him, and honoring him. He needs that. John, submit to Mary by showing her love and affection, and laying down your life by putting her first in all things. This is what she needs." That is exactly what Paul does here. This is mutual submission. And this is where it gets interesting. Look at what Paul says to husbands in Ephesians 5:25-28:

> Husbands, love your wives, just as Christ loved the church
> and gave himself up for her to make her holy . . . in this same
> way husbands ought to love their wives as their own bodies.

Now, I want you to think about the culture of their time again. Remember, wives were already expected to be slave-like and inferior to husbands (Keener, 164-66). Therefore verse 22 is actually not radical at all. For Paul to exhort women to submit to husbands, because all Christians should submit to one another, is nothing new. People of that day would not have taken note of that. What would have stood out would have been the command for men to give themselves up for their wives! That was extremely radical for that culture (Keener, 166)! "Paul . . . calls on husbands to love their wives in such a radical way that husbands become their wives' servants too" (Keener, 166).

Why is this important to understand? We read these verses in Ephesians and what stands out in bold letters to us is that women should submit to men—and then we translate that to mean they are inferior. However, Paul's intention was so far from that. "In our culture, his exhortation to wives to submit stands out more strongly; in his culture, the exhortation for husbands to love, rather than normal advice to rule the home, would have stood out more strongly" (Keener, 167). The amazing thing is that Paul tells the husband nothing about how to lead or rule—and wouldn't he if that were the role of the husband he was trying to promote? Wouldn't he outline how men are supposed to make all the decisions, run the family, and lead the inferior wife? Instead he talks only about laying down his life for his wife. Radical.

Have you ever noticed how we are to love our wives? It says, "as Christ loved the church." How did Christ love the church? He died for us (1 John 3:16). Matthew 20:28 declares, "the Son of Man did not come to be served, but to serve, and to give His life as a ransom for many." You see, when many people they read the Ephesians passage, they like to think of Christ as the King—and argue that husbands are to rule their wives as Christ is the King of the church. However, that is not the context of this verse at all. This whole text is about submission from verse 21 on. "Indeed, Christ's love is explicitly defined in this passage in terms of self-sacrificial service, not in terms of his authority" (Keener, 167). This is the profound power of that statement to husbands. It is indeed challenging in today's culture—but in the culture it was written, it was downright revolutionary. He was totally bucking the entire culture of that day!

Furthermore, it is also seen, from the reference in verse 31 about the two becoming one flesh, that this verse is not about authority, but is about one-ness and mutual submission (Keeener, 168)—the radical, culture-altering idea of mutual submission. This is what we need to learn from this Scripture. These verses were not intended to suppress women, or to make them obedient to their husbands as slaves and children were. These verses were meant to create an atmosphere of mutual submission between equal partners in marriage.

Conclusion

From the verses we have studied in the NT it can be clearly seen that nowhere does any Scripture command obedience from wives, or declare the inferiority of wives in marriage. In fact, much evidence points to a unified front between equals. It is a spiritual relationship, an organic connection, between head and body. It is not an example of hierarchical authority, but of the Biblical understanding of source and origin. It is a relationship in which the Christian rule of submission to all Christians is carried out as both partners submit to one another in Godly marriage. This is exactly the picture that was first created in Genesis. Adam was the source of Eve. And Eve was created to be the powerful equal. Called by God to rule and have dominion alongside of her husband. I am not promoting anything about women being above men, just as I do not think men should be above women. The Scripture paints a perfect picture of men and women, joined as one in unified partnership, declaring the complete image of God. It teaches us that mutual submission is the God-intended way for marriage to operate.

I want to challenge you to re-look at how you view marriage. And before you get too serious into a relationship, do some serious soul searching and Scripture study and prayer about this topic. Maybe what you have always believed in not necessarily the whole truth. Maybe you have been reading the Bible through the glasses that you have been given over the years, which in fact are inaccurate. I know this takes some study—some looking deep into the meaning of the Scripture—but isn't that worth it?

If you wrote a book, wouldn't you want people to take time to find out what you really meant when you wrote it rather than just making their own ideas based on a few statements taken out of context? Don't we owe that to God? And lastly, what and who are we committed to? Are we committed to our theology, our denomination, our past . . . or our God and his Truth? I am not trying to be overly dramatic here, but sometimes we need to lay everything down that we have believed and honestly ask the Lord to show us the Truth of the Scripture instead of men's doctrines. I pray that at the very least, this chapter will challenge you to seriously rethink these issues, even if it doesn't change your mind.

Why is This Important in a Dating Book?
There are several reasons why this is crucial for dating. First, you need to make sure you are on the same page concerning this topic before you get too serious. Imagine a woman who believed she was going to be an equal partner with her husband, trying to relate as he attempts to lead through the classical "head of household" model. Both would be unhappy and very much in conflict. As you begin to get serious in your relationship, this must be something that is thoroughly discussed.

Second, I think men and women should be practicing this in dating, before they get married. Sometimes we can make relationships all about what we can get out of them. But as we have seen, God does not intend that to be our attitude towards marriage. We are to see ourselves as servants of each other. This can begin in dating. Begin to lay down your lives for each other. Begin to look for each other's interests ahead of your own. Learn how to not be selfish, but to be giving in the relationship. Learn how to meet each other's needs, rather than always trying to make sure yours are met (all within safe scriptural boundaries, of course).

Third, I think that equality should be practiced in dating as well. Part of dating is obviously getting to know each other and finding out if you are compatible. How does the partnership work in your relationship? Can you work together? Can you treat each other well? Can you talk and listen to each other as partners, or does one always have to dominate? Do you both get your needs met? Do you both get a chance to speak into the relationship? Do you both get an opportunity to challenge the other person spiritually?

My Encouragement To Those Who Want Partnership Marriage
I think that it is so hard for women to feel that they can honestly be equal partners. Many Christian women feel guilty when they try to do this, because they feel somehow they are breaking God's special order of things. But if we can have faith in the Word of God we can begin to defeat that mentality. We can begin to see women free to use the gifts that God has given them. So many women are under the power of self-hatred and insecurity. They feel they can't do anything right, they feel unworthy of God, unworthy of love, and unable to minister God's power. I believe that a ton of this is driven by our mistaken theology about women and wives. Imagine if someone told you that God thought you were second-class!! That is essentially what Christianity has done to women for years. And we are seeing the repercussions now. I think so many women would be free of their suffering, if only men would begin to truly stand up for the truth and set our

women free. It will be hard. There will be opposition. But God's intentions are often met with such. We are called to persevere and prevail.

Lastly, I want to say that partnership marriage is something that takes effort. That is why you want to know what you believe in the Scripture. I actually think it would be easier in practice if Mandy and I lived in the traditional model of marriage. Authority and decision-making would seemingly be more clear cut. However, I know that there is so much more life, for us, in this model. I see her growing and becoming more herself, and getting free of things that hold her down as I lay my life down for her. And I see myself becoming more confident, and being stretched in the Lord by who she is as she lays down her life for me. It is truly an amazing thing. So I want to encourage you, as I end this chapter, to take an honest look at your relationship, pray about how God could revolutionize it, and set you free.

Small Group Discussion Questions:

Why is it important for a couple to discuss their own ideas of how the roles of men and women are defined in marriage?

At what point in a relationship do you think is a good time to have this discussion?

What have you been taught about the roles of men and women in marriage? What does it look like in your family?

Have you thought about how you will want to define these roles when you are married? If so, what ideas have you had?

Do you agree with Christian's definition of "headship" as being a "source or origin" rather than ruling power? Does this change your perspective on what "headship" means for a man in marriage?

At the end of this chapter, Christian talks of how both husband and wife are commanded in different ways to "submit" to one another. Can you describe in your own words what this submission would look like in a marriage?

Is it possible for two people to be mutually submitted to one another? Or do you think a family needs to have a single "leader?"

[9]

How do I know if our relationship is going well?

Telltale signs of a healthy relationship

In previous chapters we have discussed many negative characteristics of unhealthy relationships, which should be telltale signs that something must change. In this chapter, I would like to look at the same sort of idea, but from the opposite side. What are some positive characteristics we should be looking for and expecting in a healthy relationship? In other words, how can you know you are headed in the right direction?

This chapter is a list of positive characteristics compiled from my experience as well as advice I received during my dating years. This may feel a little like watching commercials, because you will read many points, without a whole lot of elaboration. The reason for this is that many are fairly self-explanatory. My hope in writing this chapter is that you can take these ideas and apply them to your relationship objectively, or ask others to do this for you, and get some idea of how things are going.

Looking for good fruit is clearly a Biblical principle, and should be applied to everything in our lives, not just dating. In Matthew 7:15-20 Jesus talks about how we will know a tree by its fruit. He says, basically, that we can tell an apple tree by the apples growing on it, and an orange tree by the oranges it grows. In the same way we should be able to look at anything in life and tell whether it is producing "good" and godly fruit, or whether it is producing bad fruit. Jesus goes on to say that "every tree that does not bear good fruit is cut down . . ." Clearly he is talking about eternal life here, but I believe we can take that verse and apply it to our lives. If anything in our life is not producing good fruit, we should cut it down!

Now, there are obvious ways to judge this. Sinning together, or driving each other away from Jesus rather than closer to Jesus, are clearly bad fruits. However, in relationships there are often more intangible "fruits" that are equally as important. In my life, I remember one day having a conversation with a trusted friend of mine who had been married for a couple years. This was while Mandy and I were still early in our dating relationship, and my friend was asking me questions to see how our relationship was going. It struck me when she asked—"Do you feel the urge to do creative stuff for her? Do you make things for her?" At first I was thinking, "What does this have to do with love?" But I then realized that this is truly a sign that you really do love someone. It is not the only sign of course, but at the time it was an encouraging one for me. It is one example from my life of an "intangible fruit." All of the intangible fruits together make up a very important part of healthy relationships. Following, I will outline some more ideas for you to think about.

Amplification
I talked about this briefly in another chapter, but it is worth mentioning here. One goal I had before I met Mandy was that whomever I ended up dating, and especially marrying, would amplify my relationship with Jesus. Scripture teaches that "As iron sharpens iron, so one man sharpens another." (Proverbs 27:17). Being sharpened in our walk with Christ is the fruit of a good and healthy relationship.

I knew, before Mandy, that to join my heart with someone, and eventually my life, would mean that Jesus would have to be the center of our relationship since he is the center of my life. Therefore, our relationship would have to increase, not hinder, my relationship with Jesus. I saw it like plugging a guitar into an amplifier—this relationship should only serve to make my Christianity stronger and able to reach more people.

After Mandy and I had been dating for a long time, I began to think over this principle. I was praying about whether she was the one I wanted to marry or not, and so I questioned her faith and relationship with Jesus— was it what I was looking for? And more importantly, did she challenge me? Did she make me a better Christian? The answer was yes. She often prayed for me, shared insights from the Bible that she was learning with me, and (maybe most importantly—if you ask people who know me) she was not afraid to stand up to me. She definitely was iron strong enough to sharpen me! I am the kind of person who has strong opinions and will argue them to the death. Mandy, in her loving way, handles this so well. She challenges me to look at almost everything from a different angle. I love that about her.

I also had to ask myself, "Do I challenge her? Do I make her want to be a better Christian?" I would also ask her if I challenged her, and I would proactively try to bless her. I would pray for her on a regular basis in my own times with God, and I would try to encourage her as often as I could (of course I still continue these practices in our marriage!).

Since that time I have been amazed by Mandy. She has turned out to be more than I ever would have imagined. I know this is just like God. He loves to go above what we can think or even imagine (Eph 3:20). Mandy challenges me, not just with words now, but also with her actions. I have seen a living, real Christianity in her that I truly admire. The truths that I stand up in front of hundreds of people and teach, she demonstrates through her life with loving kindness. It is amazing. Her gentleness, amazing prayer perseverance, and sacrificial spirit challenge me to the core. It is great. So I encourage you to find someone who sharpens you. It will make your life and marriage a constant growing experience towards Jesus.

Preferring One Another

This is a huge concept for a couple to put into action. I write a lot about this in the next chapter, but it fits here too. Selfishness, manipulation for personal gain, and looking out for yourself are all bad signs in a relationship. If you are in a relationship where the other person is more concerned with what they are getting out of it than what they can give into it, just think of what that marriage will look like! But a good sign in a relationship is when you see that your partner genuinely puts you first. He or she truly wants to see you excel, believes in your dreams, and often purposefully puts your interests first.

I talked to a friend recently who told me something his prospective girlfriend said to him. He had shared some plans for the future that he had—some dreams he hoped to chase in his life—and the girlfriend began to downplay them all as bad ideas. The reason she was doing this is that these dreams of his didn't match up exactly with what she pictured for her ideal life to look like. So she was trying to shape his dreams to fit hers. This is scary.

If that was beginning to happen in dating, think about how manipulative and controlling that person is going to be in marriage! And I have seen it coming from both the girl and the guy. The key is to prefer one another. A good sign in a relationship is if both are willing to sacrifice for the other's dreams. Your partner should be excited about your dreams; encouraging you to pursue them; offering to help in some way; and praying for God to open doors. This is a healthy and godly way to have a relationship and is a good sign that you are headed down the right road.

I know another couple who recently got engaged. They have very different pursuits and ambitions in life, which in some cases could potentially cause conflict. But these two are so dedicated to each other's dreams, that I am convinced they will seldom have conflict in this area. Their commitment is extreme at times. One is willing to move to another state for the other, one is willing to sacrifice certain job aspirations. All of this must be taken in balance so it does not become unhealthy, but this couple lives a model of laying down their lives for each other.

Let me tell you another story about Mandy. A year ago I was offered an opportunity to coach a varsity girls soccer team. For years this had been a silent dream of mine. Mandy knew it though. I had been coaching on and off for seven years, and had always hoped to reach that level. When the offer was made, Mandy knew the cost. It meant for two seasons I would be away a good deal—on top of the time I already had to be away as a pastor and traveling minister. This was a sacrifice for Mandy. She knew it. She knew it would be hard for me to be away more hours—but she also knew my dream. She told me that although it would be hard, she wanted me to do it, because she knew how much it meant to me.

Then as we got into the season, I did not achieve goals I had set for our team. Namely we didn't win as much as I'd hoped! Mandy, through and through, constantly believed in me, put up with my anxiety over the season, and constantly encouraged me in my ability as a coach. She offered, in a living example, what it means to put someone else's interests before your own. If you are missing this in your relationship, ask yourself why? What does this tell you about your partner?

Healthy Independence

Have you ever seen a couple in which both people totally lose their identities and morph into some weird uni-person? Do you know what I mean? If you were friends with one of these people before the awful disfigurement you are now asking yourself, "Where did he go? He used to be so fun, now everything is about ___." Something very unhealthy is happening when two people lose their identities, personal goals, dreams, personalities, and desires in a relationship. Yes, when you enter into a relationship things will change. You will not have as much time to hang out with your friends as you did before. Yes, at times your thoughts will be consumed with this other person. But there must be a balance. It is important that you spend time apart from each other. It is important that you spend time with your friends (of both sexes) and that the other person is OK with that and does not become insanely jealous.

So, one thing I look for as a sign for a healthy relationship is a healthy amount of distance and independence. I know that sounds counter-intuitive, but it is important. Even in marriage, when you literally become one, you still retain your own personalities and goals and dreams. God did not intend for one person's desires to overtake or consume the other's. So think about it while you are dating. Try to maintain that healthy balance. It will be good for both of you to continue to pursue your goals and dreams, and to spend time with other people. It will in fact make your relationship stronger.

That leads me to another point. I get uncomfortable when people throw away their dreams because of their boyfriend or girlfriend. In fact I get uncomfortable when people do that in marriage, but even more so in dating. When you are married, sometimes dreams do have to be put on hold for a while. However, in dating, aspirations and dreams should not be put on hold. There is not the commitment and responsibility of marriage. Therefore, you should not be throwing stuff away. Each person should still pursue his or her dreams. What if you throw away your dream, and then a year down the road you break-up. What then? Unless you are certain you are going to get married, the marriage is imminent (not 5 years away), and you sincerely feel that this dream or aspiration will not work with getting married (like becoming a monk, or something less extreme) then I think you should pursue your dreams. Even if it means spending time away from the person—it is good for you.

Security Without the Other Person

Some people find their self-worth and sense of security in having someone love them. Often you will find these people never without a significant other. This sort of living is often the result of deep wounding from the past; however it is still something that takes you away from Jesus. We are called to make Jesus our sole dependency and to rely on him for our sense of self-worth and security.

We need to look out for this in the midst of relationships as well. Ask yourself if your confidence and security for the future are wrapped up in this person in your life. Are you trusting God still, or have you begun to place your hopes and dreams in a person? Do you understand what I am getting at here? It is a good sign in a relationship if both people are able to feel secure and have self-worth on their own, and do not rely on the affection, approval, or attention of the other person to get these feelings. God intends to bring together two independently strong and faithful children of his into a healthy relationship. He does not mean to create an unequal relationship. So check yourself and your relationship, to make sure that there is no undue neediness that could cause major problems.

Fun

This may seem a little trite to some, but for me it is hugely important. Do you genuinely have fun together? Do you laugh a lot when you are together? Do you look forward to spending time together and doing things—both planned things and everyday life things? This is a very good sign. You may be thinking that you would never get into a relationship in the first place that was not fun. That seems true, but I am surprised by how many people, because of their need for someone to love them, or for the social status that it brings, will end up with someone whom they do not genuinely enjoy.

Is your relationship in general fun and peaceful, or has it become a burden? Every relationship goes through times that are particularly burdensome, but in general a healthy relationship should be a repose from the stresses of life. I know that when I come home to Mandy, I am coming home to peace, acceptance, love, and joy. Sometimes when I walk in the door after a long day, I will actually sigh because I know that I am home—and Mandy makes it such a great place for me to leave my worries behind, be myself, laugh and have fun.

Is your relationship fun—does it bring life to you? Great! It should. You should walk away from spending time together feeling rejuvenated, not feeling drained or spent. I remember times when Mandy and I would talk until three in the morning, and when I would drive home, even though I was physically tired, I still felt happy and excited and full of joy. It was just great to be together. And I could not wait to see her the next day! I would sit in class at college just thinking about what we were going to do that night— where we were going to eat, what movie we were going to see, whose house we would go to, etc.

Fun together should not be defined by what you do, but simply by the fact that you are together. If you feel the need to always be doing something huge, like going to a movie, going to an amusement park, taking trips, and so on—then maybe you should consider just doing nothing. This is actually somewhat hard for me, because I am the kind of person who always is doing something. But with Mandy, there would be days where we would just go walk outside for a long time and talk, or just hang out at home, drink hot chocolate and be together. I think healthy relationships are ones where you can have fun even doing nothing—even doing stupid things. Mandy makes things fun for me—I don't need to find things to make being with her fun. With that said, it is also very important to do special things together. I am not saying you should avoid those, I am just saying you should not have to rely on them for fun, but they are still vital to a great relationship. We love doing special things like going out to dinner, or having a picnic, or going to a concert.

My main point here is that fun is a good sign of a healthy relationship. You should be having tons of fun together. The ability to have fun in any situation will make you strong as a couple to get through the tough times. There are times when Mandy and I will be arguing and pretty upset with each other, and suddenly one of us will just start laughing because we will realize how ridiculous we are. Life is hard sometimes, and we have to be able to have fun and laughter to get through it.

Attraction

I wrote extensively about this in the chapter on creating a profile. I do want to include it here, but in a less drawn out fashion. Mainly I just want to re-iterate that it is a great sign if you are attracted to one another. You should not feel bad about this, it is a very important part of a relationship.

Now when I talk about attraction, I am not talking about some standard set by the world in all their style magazines. Attraction is about each individual, not about meeting society's norms. Please hear me on this. I think that society's norms are so skewed, and certainly we should not just look for the "perfect" looking person. What I am saying is that for you, as an individual, you must find someone to whom you are genuinely attracted. If you get married, you'll have to look at this person for the rest of your life!! You better like what you are looking at!

More Than Just a Physical Relationship

I know I am supposed to be talking about positive things here—but this one is more of a caution. I felt it was necessary to put this in here, because I have seen couples get so enamored with the physical side of their relationship that they miss out on the more important aspects like talking. A good sign for your relationship is if you can keep this part of your relationship in balance. It should be the lowest priority in dating. Once the physical part of the relationship becomes the center, you will find that you have a hard time talking, knowing much about each other, and staying away from sin. You need to keep this part of the relationship in check to ensure the healthy growth of your relationship.

Creativity—Desire To Do Things For Each Other

Do you feel like doing special things for each other? Do you want to make things for each other, like songs, mix CD's, photos, paintings, poems ...etc? This is a good sign. Even to this day, having been married almost five years, I still get excited when I get an idea to make something that I know she'll love. There is just something about putting a lot of effort into something that you know will have some special meaning to the person you love.

Now, not everyone is amazingly creative, but the principle still holds true. The whole idea is that if you are truly invested in this person then you will want to do things to make him or her happy. You will have an idea of what they love, and be willing to put time and energy into it. An example that isn't creative in an artistic sense comes from something Mandy did several years back. I am a drummer, and I love this group named STOMP. They do incredible percussion with all sorts of weird "instruments" like trash can lids and PVC pipe. They came to a city near us while we were dating, and Mandy, knowing how much I love them, surprised me with tickets to go see them. This was amazing! It was an incredible gift. And what made it so special was that it showed two things; (1) she knew me well—my desires that maybe others wouldn't have been so sensitive to and (2) she spent time on something just for me. That is so cool isn't it?

I could tell you tons of stories like this. Remember that coaching job I told you about a couple of paragraphs ago? Well, I recently had to give up that job (which I loved) because we now have two children, and my workload at church has become more substantial. The day after this decision was final, I found a big card made from construction paper taped to the door when I got home. There was a soccer ball on the front and it said "Coach Dada." My oldest boy, Samuel, had done a lot of amazing drawings all over it, and on the inside Mandy had written a note "from the boys" saying how excited they were that I would be able to coach them this spring instead! I know that sounds little, but those are the special kinds of things that show that someone loves you. It is more than being creative. It is showing how invested you are in this person's life. It is showing that you care about what they think, how they feel, and what they want. Doing creative things for each other is a good sign for a relationship.

I realize the only two stories I shared have been about Mandy. But I want to emphasize that not only the women are supposed to do these special creative things. Guys, you are not off the hook! When we dated I took great pride in the many creative ways I showed Mandy my love for her. One of my greatest moments came after we got engaged. We got engaged in a state park where this tree had fallen and made the perfect place to sit. For her birthday I went back and took a picture of this place with the sun setting and shining beautifully through the trees. Then I had my friend who was good with design, scan the picture in and write a verse of Song of Solomon that I had read to her when I asked her to marry me. I then took it to a frame shop run by a friend of mine and had it professionally framed. It is beautiful, and it still hangs in our house!

Genuine Interest in Things You Do

When Mandy and I began to get serious I quickly realized that she liked what I call "country crafts." She liked to go to stores or craft shows and just look at all these little crafty things. She loved to buy them and take them home and show them to her sister and mom. They loved them too. They would "oohh" and "aaahh" and talk about how much they liked it. Sometimes it felt like they were on a different planet than me!

I had never bought anything like that. I had never understood it much. But once I fell in love with Mandy, I learned! I used to buy her crafts like they were going out of style (they did with Mandy, finally!). We used to drive to go look at crafts at special outlets and shop for the perfect "basket." You see, crafts were not very important to me, but Mandy was. Therefore, crafts became important too.

This is one way to love each other—invest in the other person's interests, even if it does not make much sense to you. Mandy often watches football with me. It is not her normal idea of fun, but she will watch with me because she loves me.

It goes even deeper than this though. I once knew this couple where the girl was a great dancer and a great musician. The guy was a worship leader and musician and really loved music. I remember one day talking with her about how things were going and she shared with me that he had recently made some weird comments. He had started challenging her on her dancing. You see, she was so good that she was going to college for it. He, however, was hoping (in my opinion) that she would abandon dance for music so they could do music together. During their relationship he never once attended a performance of hers. He often intimated that he thought doing music in ministry would be much more worthy of her time and energy.

This showed me that he did not have a genuine interest in something that was hugely important to her, and consequently he did not have a real genuine interest in her either. If someone you are with is not willing to invest time and energy into things that are important to you, do not just excuse it. It is important. Love should be about supporting one another and believing in one another. It is hard to fight for your dreams and to be who you are called to be. When you join your life to someone else, you need that person to be helpful and not a hindrance. A godly husband or wife will speak encouragement to you and believe in you, even if it is in an area that is not personally interesting to them. This is why it is so important to see it happening in dating. If it is not happening, and you are seriously dating each other, then chances are it will never begin to happen. They may think that you are there to serve their dreams. They may not think your dreams are as challenging as theirs, so they do not respect them. Either way, it would be a frustrating marriage to say the least, to be married to someone who would not take the time to invest in your interests and dreams. So be aware of this in dating, and ask God for discernment.

Not Trying to Change You
This point is implied in the previous discussion, but is worth directly mentioning. A sign that someone is treating you right and loving you with God's love is if they love you for who you are now. I am not saying that they should not challenge you to grow. That is crucial too. But when one person begins to try and change the other person to better fit their "ideal" it gets dangerous. You want someone to love you for who you are, and for who they see God is making you to be. You do not want someone who loves you for who they think they can make you to be. There is balance here, because we all need refining, and the ones we love the most will often be the best agents for that. However, when one person tries to encourage change in

another so that they will fit a certain mold, that is disrespecting that person's free will as well as God's creative influence in that person's life.

Agreement / Able to Disagree

Again, we are looking for another balance here in a healthy relationship. A good sign for a relationship is if there is a lot of agreement. It is a bad sign (obviously I think) if you are always disagreeing and arguing about everything. If you can't walk in unity now, why assume you will be able to for the rest of your lives? But I also feel that it would be unhealthy to always agree in everything. To me, that would show a lack of honesty with each other.

The ability to disagree with each other is powerful. And how each person handles it will determine if it bears good fruit. When you disagree, do you fight? Does one person always win? Does one person sulk when they don't get their way? Or can you find a balance of maintaining unity while still disagreeing? This is crucial. Learning how to deal with conflict between each other, and not letting it become something that comes between you, is vital for dating. To be married you need to see yourself as a team. That is why, even in disagreement, there needs to be some sense of unity. Look at your relationship (if and when you are in one) and see if this balance exists.

I am not saying that you will never have arguments. But I am saying that in the end you need to be able to come together in unity. Mandy and I have had our share of disagreements where we have not acted like "a team" the whole time. However, in the end we are always able to come together, ask forgiveness for where we went wrong, and talk out our feelings. Even in topics where we do disagree, we are able to express why we disagree, and how it makes us feel, and then come to a place of understanding. This is important because in the end we (our relationship, our love for one another) are more important than the issue. Our unity is critical for our marriage, for us as individuals, and for our children.

Vulnerability / Honesty (In Healthy Amounts If Just Dating)

Being able to share your hearts with one another is clearly an important part of dating and relationships. Knowing when and how much to share can be tricky. Some people have a hard time opening up. If that is you, then this section is about the need for every person to have people in their lives with whom they can be vulnerable. Depending on how serious you get, this should include the person you are dating. The place that I have seen the most problems, though, is not people who are reluctant to share, but people who share way too much, way too early. It is like we have no self-control, or at least no idea what is reasonable and appropriate to share, and what should be kept to ourselves. I see people sharing some deep things in their heart, and if it comes too early, it can freak the other person out, and often tear down the relationship. It can also lead to an inappropriate bonding that is truly too deep for the stage of relationship they are in.

So how do we balance this? I have a principle that may help you. It comes from Matthew 12:34 which says, "Out of the overflow of the heart, the mouth speaks." Try to apply this to dating. The commitment in your heart should determine the honesty of your mouth. In other words, the amount of honesty you give in a relationship should be directly proportionate to the amount of commitment in your heart you feel towards that person. For instance, if you are talking about getting engaged, then most likely you are very committed already to each other. This kind of commitment puts you in a place where you both should be sharing very deeply with each other. However if you have only been together a little while, and only have a limited level of commitment to each other, then you should consciously limit the amount of personally deep things that you share with one another.

The danger of sharing too much too early is that you risk getting hurt. If you give the treasures of your heart to someone in a context where there is no true commitment, you are opening yourself up to pain. Commitment brings safety. Marriage is the ultimate commitment, and therefore Mandy knows that her feelings, thoughts, fears, and dreams are completely safe with me. And since she is safe, she can be totally honest. When we were dating though, and I had not decided whether I knew I wanted to marry her, I could only offer her so much commitment—and therefore only so much safety. She knew this (and it went both ways) and as a result would not share some things with me until much further along in our relationship.

Not only do you open yourself up to being hurt, but once you are hurt, this will begin to breed in you a false fear of intimacy. What I mean by that is you will think, "I opened up . . .I got hurt . . . I am not going to open up again and let myself be hurt." But you see, it is a false fear because you did not open up in a truly committed and safe place. God will provide for you someone with whom all the treasures of your heart will be safe. You just need to be patient and wise. It is hard, I know. When you are excited about being "in love" with someone, you want to tell them everything. That is natural, and actually a very good sign. But, you need to have some self-control. It will be better for both of you, and for your relationship, if you take your time and wisely reveal your heart, rather than pouring it all out at once. I know I have used this verse already in this book, but it is good to remember for this too:

> Do not give dogs what is sacred; do not throw your pearls to
> pigs. If you do, they may trample them under their feet, and
> then turn and tear you to pieces (Matthew 7:6).

I am not trying to say that the person you are in love with is a dog or a pig, but the principle here is to not put your treasure in the hands of people you do not know you can trust, or else you could be torn to pieces.

Go Through Hard Times Together

This, I have found through talking to my friends, is something that I firmly believe in. It is not because I love hard times, it is because I believe that people are great deceivers, even when we are not trying to be. What I mean is that we can all "look good" when we need to, but when things get difficult is when we show our true selves. I write at length about this in the chapter on finding the one, but I just want to mention this here. A good sign, a good fruit to look for in your relationship, is if you can weather good and bad times together. The bad times could be relationship troubles, or they could be problems in one or the other person's lives, or circumstantial problems. Whatever it is, if you can last through pressure, that is a great sign. And not only "last" but if you can fall more in love, find more that you like about each other, or find that you love each other despite some of the bad things you might have found out during the bad times. That is very good. Do you like what you see in each other when you are under stress and not trying to be on your best behavior? Do you admire each other in difficult times, or do you think—"Wow, she does not handle these things well. I am glad she is not always like this!"

I know that for me, a huge turning point in my dating relationship with Mandy was when we had a sort-of break up. I had hurt her feelings pretty badly and we needed to "take a break" for a while. During this time we both showed each other some very raw emotions. And we pretty much saw what the bottom of the barrel would look like for each other. In this, I saw Mandy overcome something. As a result of our little break up we realized that we both needed counseling before we could even consider marriage. Mandy had always had an aversion to counseling. Trusting people is sometimes difficult for her, and counseling is trusting someone with the deepest parts of your emotions. So this was not something she wanted to do. But in this time I saw Mandy make a decision that she needed counseling— and what was cool is she didn't do it for me, she did it for herself. And she ended up loving it, and allowing God to change her.

I have to say, after all the many reasons I had already found to love her, this sent me over the top. I saw in Mandy, even in the midst of turmoil, uncertainty, and doubt, a desire to be humble and submissive to God's voice. I saw that nothing was more important to her than God's will in her life. Not even her love for me, or her fear of trusting people. God came first, and she desperately wanted Him to have total freedom to work in her life. When I saw this part of Mandy's character, it was the last straw. It was the missing piece that my heart had been waiting for before I could say, "I know you are the one." So I encourage you to see how each other goes through hard times. It will be an excellent indicator.

Taking an Honest Approach

I know it may be weird to read a whole chapter like this and try to analyze a relationship that you are in. I know, in some ways, it feels like it isn't that romantic. It may feel almost like you are betraying each other, trying to analyze the relationship, as well as the other person. But this is so crucial. This is by far the most important decision you will ever make in your life (besides becoming a Christian) and it will have the most far-reaching implications in every area of your life, for the rest of your life. So many people make this decision based on one or two factors, often just feelings. I think wisdom is to be patient and take your time and know what you are getting into.

So while it may feel a little un-romantic to do this, I strongly encourage you to honestly take inventory of your relationship periodically to see if you are growing apart, or growing together. Look at whether you are feeling more and more like this person is someone you want to spend the rest of your life with, or less and less. And look for healthy fruit. We are imperfect people. And many of us are wounded people. It is very easy for our hearts to go towards someone who is not good for us. You may have unbelievably strong feelings, and great times together, but if you are honest about the fruit, you might see that it is not of God. On the other hand, if you do see a lot of great fruit, that can be one more confirmation as you make your decision. In the following few chapters, we will talk at length about other ways to come to a faith and a peace about whether your relationship is one meant for, and ready for, marriage.

Small Group Discussion Questions:
What can you do to create an atmosphere of "amplification" in your
relationship, instead of it becoming a distraction?

Below is a list of all the "signs" of a healthy relationship from this chapter.
Read over them and discuss which ones strike you as the most important to
you. Which ones are you really hoping to see in a relationship?

Amplification
Preferring One Another
Healthy Independence
Security Without the Other Person
Fun
Attraction
More Than Just a Physical Relationship
Creativity
Genuine Interest in the Things You Do
Not Trying to Change You
Agreement/Able to Disagree
Vulnerability/Honesty (in healthy amounts if just dating)
Go Through Hard Times Together

If you are in a relationship (or if you've ever been in one) which one(s) are the
most challenging for you?

Are there any on this list that you disagree with? Is there anything that you
think should be added to this list? If so, describe it.

Do you think that a couple must go through some hard times together to
really know if they belong together? What if hard times have never really
presented themselves? Does that mean that couple is not ready to move
forward?

Here's a question to work on by yourself, not in a group setting: If you are
already in a relationship, take some time to look over this list and prayerfully
score each one on a scale of 1-5 (1 = low and 5 = high). Be honest as you
examine your relationship. After doing this, talk with someone you trust
about your strengths and weaknesses as a couple. Is there anything that you
should work on?

How do I know if I am in love?

What true love looks like

You cannot write a book about dating without dealing with this question, right? What is true love? How will I know it when I am in love? How will I know if someone else is in love with me? I recently taught about dating to a large college group, and someone came up to me afterwards saying he thought the word "love" carried more power than I realized. I had told people it was OK to tell someone you loved them before you got engaged. However, he argued that many people use these words so frivolously that they only end up in hurt and pain. If this is true, is there a right time to tell someone you love them? And how long does it take true love to form?

Understanding what true love is all about is important to dating and finding the one for several reasons. First, I think whenever we get into a romantic relationship we are always trying to discover if we are truly in love. Second, I think we need to understand what we should expect from someone else—if they say they "love" us, how can we tell if it is true? And third, if we are going to tell someone, "I love you," then we need to know what that requires of us.

What is Love?

We should start at a very fundamental level here and figure out what love really is. I think that for many of us love can mean deep emotional feelings, commitment, attraction, friendship, a deep "bond," an appreciation of who the person is, and so on. All of these are good, and are part of love, but one day while reading the Bible, the Lord taught me a very strong lesson.

I John 3:16 starts off "This is how we know what love is. . ." This is great. It is essentially an introduction to a definition—it is almost the same as saying—"Love is . . ." and then outlining the definition. He goes on to describe love in this way: "Jesus Christ laid down His life for us." Simple and powerful. He laid down his life for us. What does this mean for us? I see three major aspects of love shown here: 1) Love is a Choice; 2) Love is an Action; and 3) Love is a Sacrifice.

#1) Love is a Choice

First and foremost, this verse tells us that love is a choice. Jesus was not forced to lay down his life; he was not taken by surprise or caught off guard. The reason he came into the world was to lay down his life for us. This is one reason why the Garden of Gethsemane prayer is so powerful. He asks the Father to take this cup away from him if possible, but then submits to the Heavenly Father's will and voluntarily offers his life up for ours. This is so powerful to me because it shows he had a choice. He could have chosen to refuse the cup, but he "humbled himself and became obedient to the point of death, even the death of the cross" (Phil 2:8, NKJV). For you, for me—he voluntarily made the choice to lay down his life. Why? Because he loved us (John 3:16)!

From Jesus' example we learn that love is a definite choice. What does this mean for us? First it shows us that love is not only about the feelings we feel. Love goes light-years beyond romantic feelings, moonlit dances, and special songs . . . it is about making a choice. A choice that this person is the one to whom you give yourself above everyone else in the world. This helps us in deciding whom we should date and whom we should marry. I think it shows us that we had better not make these decisions based on the evidence of our feelings alone, but we need to make sure that everything within us is at peace and confident with making this choice.

In saying this I am not saying that "feelings" are unimportant. I once heard a man who had been married for around 20 years describe his marriage. He said that when his wife and he were younger they had the strong loving feelings that we all think of when we think of love, but that after years of being together, he did not feel any strong emotions towards her other than commitment and loyalty. The excitement was gone, the passion was absent, and the feelings of love had been replaced by something he claimed was more real. This man's theory is not what I am saying about love. Feelings are essential to love throughout a relationship. How these feelings continue, though, is by choosing repeatedly throughout the relationship to love each other passionately. Through those choices the feelings of love can be nurtured and sustained, and even grow in intensity.

Understanding that love is a choice helps us get perspective on our feelings, but it does not eliminate or denigrate them. What do I mean by perspective? Our feelings, especially during the dating phase of a relationship, can become so overwhelming and consuming that we totally lose objectivity on what God wants for us. Feelings of attraction and passion can become so powerful so quickly that we can jump into saying "I love you" way before we are ready to make the commitment that those words truly require. Therefore, understanding that true love is a choice gives you perspective on your feelings and allows you to step outside of your feelings and make a good decision. When you follow your feelings alone, you are not making a decision, you are only being led by what many call your "heart." But when you understand it is a choice, it is making a statement with more than your heart—and it actually becomes more meaningful to say, "I love you." The first time I told Mandy I loved her, I was not saying, "I have lots and lots of uncontrollable feelings for you." I was saying, "I do have lots of uncontrollable feelings for you, and I also have decided that I want to make a commitment to you to see if we are meant to be together." Can you see the difference?

Therefore, while this understanding gives us perspective and makes our words more meaningful and true, it does not eliminate feelings. Feelings are a crucial and powerful part of love. Jesus shows this repeatedly throughout Scripture as he weeps, shows compassion, and heals those he loves. If you read Song of Solomon you will again see that love is meant to be full of passion and joy and excitement—"it burns like a blazing fire, like a mighty flame" (SOS 8:6). So I definitely disagree with the view of the person I told you about a couple paragraphs ago—I believe that these feelings, intense feelings, will only grow as marriage continues. Yes, loyalty and commitment grow stronger as well, but I believe married couples need to continue to fan the flame of their feelings for one another. I know many married couples, including Mandy and I, who purposefully go out on dates, even though we are married, because we need to get out of the routine of daily responsibility and just enjoy each other and have fun together. Please do not misinterpret what I am saying here to mean that feelings are less important—they simply should not be the only part of love.

The second lesson that understanding love as a choice shows me is that love is not just about the easy times. Love is easy when you are not fighting, or when there is no stress in life, or when both people are doing great in their personal lives. But when real life begins to happen, when you enter into crises, when you are tested as a couple or as individuals, what will show? Will your short temper and your selfish needs show, or will your choice to love this person no matter what show?

This is a crucial understanding for dating and for marriage. I often tell people that I hope they encounter some sort of difficult trial during their dating phase, before they get engaged. Why? Because trials reveal true character (James 1) and it is essential that you know the true character of the person you intend to marry before making such a huge decision. There is a principle that Jesus teaches about love, when he tells us to love our enemies. He says it is easy to love people who love us back—"If you do good to those who are good to you, what credit is that to you" (Luke 6:33)? The real test of love, he says, is if you can love people who do not love you back, and who are not good to you. I am not saying that we should see the people we are dating as our enemies, but I think Jesus teaches a principle here that can cross over to dating. Think of it this way: "If you love each other when you totally agree on everything, and you have nothing to argue about, and there are no major conflicts or life struggles you must endure together, what credit is that to you?" It is easy to love each other during the good times! It is during the struggles, the trials, the disagreements, and the arguments where true love is exposed for what it is—whether real or not.

Understanding that love is a choice and not solely about feelings gives you what you need to get through the trials. For instance, when I am grating on Mandy, and arguing about every petty thing, and not acting lovingly towards her—I am sure it is not her intense feelings of adoration that sustain her attitude of love towards me—right? What is it? It is her choice to love me. Her commitment that love is not about everything going right and feeling right, but love is about standing by someone's side no matter what comes your way.

Jesus' love for us portrays this more powerfully than any other example. In Romans 5:8 it says that he died for us while we were still sinners. This is so powerful. Think about it—1 John tells us that his love is shown to us in that he died for us, and Romans says he died for us while we were sinning. Therefore, when Christ decided to make the most powerful act of love in history, he did not do it for people who were already worshipping him, or for people who had treated him well. He did it for sinners—for you and me—for people who were turning their backs on him, cheating on him, and murdering him! That is so humbling and so incredible, isn't it? Surely then, Christ's love was not meant to be something that existed only in the good times, he proved to us that his love was real even when we reciprocated nothing.

I learn from Jesus' love, therefore, that true love does not exist just during "good times" but also in the midst of struggle, trial, and difficulty. This understanding is pivotal for dating relationships. This can answer the question of whether you truly love somebody, or whether somebody truly loves you. Are they willing to make the choice through the hard times? Are you? What does that say about your love? These are good and important questions to ask yourself when you are trying to figure out whether you are truly in love with someone.

#2) Love is An Action: Love is Patient, Kind . . . . Are You?
When Christ laid down his life for us, not only was it a choice, but it was an outward expression of his love for us. His love was more than just words; he put it into action. An obvious way to describe love is found in 1 Corinthians 13:4-8:

> Love is patient, love is kind. It does not envy, it does not boast, it is not proud. It is not rude, it is not self-seeking, it is not easily angered, it keeps no record of wrongs. Love does not delight in evil but rejoices in the truth. It always protects, always trusts, always hopes, always perseveres.

Look at that list. I see a list of choices that result in action. When Mandy is having a hard day, but I am tired and I do not want to take the time to help her out around the house, I have a choice to be kind. It does not just happen because I love her. I choose it, because I choose to love her. Each of these characteristics comes from an internal choice you make, every time, to love someone, and results in an external action.

If you are "feeling impatient," that is a lie. You are simply choosing to be impatient. This is a powerful principle in my marriage. I have learned many ways in which to make Mandy feel loved by me, and they are not always conventional. For instance, one night recently I wanted to have a quiet time with the Lord, but the kitchen was messy and I knew that Mandy had plans the next morning, so she would be overloaded if she had to do the kitchen too. I tried to start praying, but God brought this verse to my mind about love—and I realized that love is not just a feeling I can say that I have for Mandy if there is no fruit. The fruit is a decision I make that produces an action that blesses her. So I got up and cleaned for 30 minutes. I not only did the dishes, but also scrubbed the counters, put away dishes, washed down the table, organized some papers, put away our kids' toys, and then went to bed, knowing that I had just loved my wife, and in fact loved God also.

It helps me to know that love is a choice, and that the list in Corinthians is full of choices, because then I do not stand around waiting to feel like doing things. Instead I make a decision to be proactive in my loving, and to let my love be shown through action. I John 3:18 says,

> Dear children, let us not love with words or tongue but with actions and truth.

We need to apply this verse to our relationships. It is important to note that this must be applied by both the male and the female in the relationship. Depending on whom you talk to, some will emphasize the need for sacrifice more from one or the other. However in true Biblical unity, both partners must do this for each other for it to be true love.

I know I continue to say the same thing, but true love is not wrapped up solely in emotions. True love must be evidenced through action. This, again, is important for dating relationships. If someone says they love you, how can you know? Judge them by their actions. Do their actions line up with their words? If they say they love you, do their actions show commitment, sacrifice, and putting you first? If not, do they truly love you? It is easy to say, "I love you." It is much harder to live it.

Sometimes I look around and I see people who have such low expectations for what love should look like. We allow people to simply throw these words around without ever backing it up. People promise love, and move into physical intimacy, without ever truly walking in a relationship of love. I overheard some teenagers in the mall today talking about how they thought they might need a pregnancy test, and I thought to myself—that is so sad! What they are experiencing in their life right now is not love. It is just sex. True love would be kind and patient. True love would be wise. And all of that means that true love would not end up in sex when you are sixteen years old! I felt so bad for these girls, but we see it everyday in less obvious ways. You are in a relationship and you allow your boyfriend to talk down to you; you allow your girlfriend to manipulate you; you use the words "I love you" to get affection, intimacy, and physicality without ever putting action behind those words. Basically what I am saying is that we need to be wise judges. Test your partner's love. Is he or she patient? Does he keep a record of wrongs? How do her actions measure up to her words? This is an important test, because where people's actions fall short in dating, they will fall short even more in marriage.

#3) *Love is a Sacrifice*
This leads into the third major lesson that can be learned from 1 John 3:16. Love is a sacrifice. I have hinted at this throughout the previous sections, true love shines in the dark places. True love becomes especially evident when all the circumstances are trying to squeeze love out. The phrase that John uses, "to lay down your life," has been etched in my mind. What does it mean to lay down your life for someone? I have begun to seek out ways in which I can actively lay down my life for Mandy. And she has done the same for me.

Before I talk more about laying down your life for someone you love, first let me say this. I think there is one major obstacle that stands in the way of truly laying down our lives for people we love. The obstacle is the Western notion of personal rights. Please do not misunderstand me—I am very thankful for our rights as citizens, and for the amazing price so many people have paid to earn us those rights and protect them. But sometimes, I believe as Christians, we can become too Westernized. We are taught that we have rights to freedom, our own tastes, our own choices, basically we have rights to do and say almost anything that doesn't directly or indirectly inhibit someone else's rights. And lately there has been a surge for defending the rights of more and more groups of people. We have been indoctrinated with the idea that we "deserve" certain privileges and if we are denied them then we are being wronged in some way.

This way of thinking, although great for our society, stands in contrast with some teachings in the Bible. For instance, how would the notion of rights correspond to Jesus' teaching that if someone steals your coat, give them your clothes as well?

My point in saying all that is that sometimes our mind-set of deserving certain rights can get in the way of us truly laying down our lives for each other. For instance one ideal we hold dear is that if you perform some work, you have the right to earn something in return. Let's apply this to a relationship. For instance, assume that today Mandy did something very nice for me, like cook a special dinner for me, or surprise me with a gift of some sort. Should she do this in order to receive something in return? Or should it be a free gift of love to me?

This is why Jesus' idea of love turns the world's idea of love upside down. The world teaches if you do something good, you should demand something in return, but God teaches that if you do something good, it should be done in love as a free gift with no strings attached. Sometimes it helps me to view my love as a sacrifice that I am putting on an altar—I am not laying it there and waiting for something in return, or waiting to pick it back up again. I am truly laying it down in an act of love. My love needs to be a free gift, otherwise it can become selfish and manipulative. If I start doing good things to make the other person like me more or do good things for me it becomes manipulative and controlling.

That is why salvation is a free gift to us. Jesus is modeling for us how our love should be, not in the way of the world, but in a true laying down of your rights, your privileges, and your life for another person. Did Jesus deserve to die? No! Did he not have rights? Of course he did. But he laid them down for us. Of his own free will he gave up his rights in order to love us. The Bible tells us that we are called to consider others better than ourselves and to not look out for our interests, but also for the interests of others (Philippians 2:3-4). We are told to humble ourselves in the sight of God, and he will exalt us in due time (1 Peter 5:6). When we get the attitude that we deserve certain things, we begin to put ourselves before other people, rather than laying down our lives in love.

Talking about laying down your rights can be dangerous territory though. Some people will be tempted to take this too far, and begin to burden people with expectations that are truly unbiblical. It is true that it is not good to do sacrificial actions in order to produce some sort of action from our partner. That is selfish and often manipulative, as I have already pointed out.

However, if we never have our sacrificial actions reciprocated by our partner, that is equally as unhealthy. It is not that we should never receive anything in return, just that getting something in return should not be our motivation. We should give out of love as a free gift. But we should also receive that exact same thing from our partner. If we do not, then we are in an unhealthy relationship and in danger of being totally taken advantage of. When we lay down our lives as a free gift, that should be reciprocated by the other person equally. If it is not, then the relationship is unbalanced and one-sided. Such a relationship will result in hardship and heartache.

Let me give you another practical example. There are days when I come home and Mandy is stressed out, and as a result is more irritated and short tempered than normal. This can sometimes lead to Mandy saying things that she doesn't mean, or just being short with me in a way that hurts my feelings. In those moments, I do have rights—I do deserve to be treated better (and Mandy would be the first to agree with that). But sometimes, out of love for her, I will choose to lay down those rights and rather than confront her on her behavior, I will gently calm her down and ask her questions to bring whatever is bothering her into the light.

Self-focus is what fuels a lot of fights. If I were to think solely of myself, I would think, "I do not deserve this, she is acting wrong, she needs to change." However, when in love I lay down my rights and my life, I think something more like this—"I know she is acting in an unloving way now, but I know there is more to it, she has had a hard day. I am going to show her my love by giving her grace and helping her through this rather than confronting her right now." That is a very real way in which we can lay down our lives for each other.

Again, it is crucial to understand that all of this must happen two ways. If only one person sacrifices, that is unhealthy. It should not always be the man, and it should not always be the woman. In a healthy relationship both are doing this equally for each other. There can be no one-sided sacrifice, that always leads to greater problems. It leads to one person taking advantage of the one who sacrifices, and then that person becomes resentful and bitter. That is not what we are hoping for here. The goal is that both people greatly desire to lay down their lives for each other. Only when sacrifice is two-way, will there be true health and blessing.

Understanding the Limits of Sacrifice

Learning how to put the other person first in your relationship is vital to true love; however, there are many sad instances where this is taken too far. This is important to discuss too, because in dating it is not only important to learn how to lay down your life, but you need to know when you are being treated unfairly and need to get out. An extreme example is the many women who are battered in Christian homes, and stay in their situations because they feel they must submit to their husbands. In a less extreme example, someone might find themselves in a relationship where their needs are simply never met.

When laying down your life in an act of loving sacrifice goes too far, you must get out of the relationship. In my understanding, while we are called to love through sacrifice, there are still boundaries that we must live our lives by. We need to set these boundaries and be careful that people do not cross them. For example, a very obvious boundary that everyone should have in any relationship is that one person is not allowed to physically assault or abuse the other. If a person crosses that boundary, that is not the time to lay down your life in love, it is the time to confront, rebuke, and discipline.

That may sound harsh, but it is biblical truth. I want to take a second to make a point that some of you might think is obvious. I have heard people argue before that boundaries in Christian relationships are un-godly and unloving. Some people think that they are controlling, manipulative, and judgmental. That thought process, in my opinion, stems from an erroneous understanding of the nature of boundaries. People who view boundaries as wrong, in my opinion, feel that these boundaries are made out of pride or vengeance. However, the opposite is true—boundaries that protect yourself, or the people you love, are made out of love and stewardship (of what God has committed to your care, including your own body and spirit).

Who was the first person to make boundaries? God was! In Genesis 3 we are told of how God created a beautiful garden for Adam and Eve to enjoy, and how he had created one very simple boundary; do not eat from the tree of the knowledge of good and evil. Why did he make this boundary? Because he loved them! Throughout the history of the Bible you can watch as the Lord makes boundaries to love and protect his people, the 10 commandments being the most famous.

In the New Testament we see a similar understanding. In Matthew 18, Jesus outlines a process by which we are supposed to confront one another when we are sinned against. You may have never thought of it in this way before, but that scripture affirms the need for boundaries. Jesus is teaching us not only how to confront, but that we should confront when we are sinned against, when lines are crossed, when boundaries are broken. There would be no need to confront if boundaries did not exist and were not good and worthy of being upheld.

I know I said a lot there about something that may seem obvious, but it is so important. Please learn what healthy boundaries are for a romantic relationship. Some of you have not seen healthy boundaries in your parents' relationship, and you need to be taught. Find a mentor, or a book on healthy boundaries, or a pastor with a good marriage to teach you so that you can know what you are looking for, and how you should be treated.

Many people live under the lie that enduring mistreatment (whether verbal, emotional, physical, or sexual) is a noble and godly way to show love. This simply is not true. True love will never breed hurt, pain, isolation, and fear. The Bible teaches that true love drives out fear (1 John 4:18), it does not create it. So I encourage you to learn this about true love, and to expect it from anyone who says, "I love you." Expect to be treated right.

Everyone is Lifted Up
The idea here of '1 John 3:16 love' is that both people in a relationship are practicing this kind of love, not just one person. If only one is laying down his or her life, then this does not work the way God intended it to. That is much of what we were just discussing, in a relationship where one lays down her life, and the other takes advantage. If this is done right, however, both people will be laying down their lives for the other, and therefore both will be lifted up.

I have this picture in my mind of Mandy and I that I am lifting her up—in my words and actions I am trying to serve her ideas, her dreams, her everyday life—I am trying to lift her up, to bless her, to lay down my life and put hers first. That is a great picture. But what is cool is that she is doing the exact same thing for me. She is laying down her life to lift me up as well. In the picture I use to describe this, I see me lifting her up, and then she lifts me higher than where I just lifted her, and then I lift her higher than where she just lifted me, and so on. That is the amazing part. This principle grows upon itself. As we lay down our lives for each other, we are able to bless each other in more powerful ways, because the other person has been laying down their life for us too. The verses that back this up are great. The most powerful and telling is 1 Peter 5:5-6:

> Yes, all of you be submissive to one another, and be clothed
> with humility, for "God resists the proud, but gives grace
> to the humble." Therefore, humble yourselves under the
> mighty hand of God, that he may exalt you in due time
> (NKJV).

"All of you be submissive to one another" is so obvious. It is not hidden somewhere in the text, the truth is right there—submit to each other! Be humble! And then God's grace will be able to flow into your relationship and you will be exalted into God's plan for your life in his timing.

So, How Do You Know When You Are in Love?

I hope by now you know that feelings of love are not enough evidence to know you are in love. Being in love has several stages of decision and commitment. Most people start out with some form of attraction and infatuation, and at some point that interest grows strong enough to push them into actually spending time getting to know the other person. Through time together, feelings of attraction will often grow stronger. The real test, however, is when you come to decisions about commitment, sacrifice, and the future.

The first level of "in love" is probably pretty close to infatuation, but with a commitment to see what will happen with this person over time. That is one of the first signs of "being in love"—having the desire to focus solely on this person, spend tons of time together, seek God about the relationship, and see where it goes. The deeper levels of "in love," come when you are faced with certain transitions where you realize you will have to give up something in order to stay "in love."

For instance, let's assume you have an ideal you are looking for in a girl. You meet a girl who satisfies many of the things you were hoping for, but does not (at least to your knowledge so far) fulfill this one ideal. I think one way to know you are truly falling in love is when you come to the point where you decide—"I am going to lay down this ideal and commit to this person, even though she does not have this ideal—I love her as a person (when I say that I mean—who she is, how she treats you, how she makes you feel, what she stands for) more than my ideal."

For me, that is a big step in a relationship. When you realize that you have suddenly decided that the person you have come to know now outweighs the ideal you have formed over years. This is a great realization and has a lot to do with falling in love. Also, it does not have to be an ideal that is laid down, it could be something else in life. But when you realize you are truly willing to sacrifice because of this person, that is a form of commitment, and I think that shows a lot about love.

Along with growing commitment, falling in love will also bring an increasing desire to talk about, plan, and spend your future together. I remember that there came a time in my relationship with Mandy where I was talking to the Lord about whether I wanted to make that next step of love and commitment and ask her to marry me. I was thinking back through all the things I had wanted to find in a wife, and all that she fulfilled, plus all the new wonderful traits I had never thought of. And as I tried to be very analytical, one thought overtook my mind . . . I realized very truly, that I did not want to live without her. In fact I could not imagine living my life without her. My feelings of love were immensely strong, blinding at times, but my decision of love was all the more powerful. I decided that I wanted her in my life forever; that I could see no other option. She was it. I had finally found her!

What a great moment that was! And to this day that same feeling and that decision ring even stronger. I am so in love with the "person" of Mandy, and all that she brings to every area and facet of my life, that I cannot imagine being without her. My life, and myself, would be incomplete. And that is what marriage is all about—becoming one. This is a pretty big point, and I want to end this chapter with it. I think falling in love also has a lot to do with finding someone with whom you "fit together." Someone who truly does complete you. You get the feeling that you are more yourself when you are with them. You find them even making you become more like you always wanted to be, and like what God wants you to be. Mandy used to say, when we were dating and getting engaged, that when she was with me, it was like "coming home." And I felt, and feel, exactly the same way. It is like finding a place you have been searching for your whole life. You have come home. You are complete. I know this is a little abstract. In the next chapter I will talk more about this. I will also share some ideas on how to know if you are ready to move from the "falling in love" stage into deeper levels of commitment.

Small Group Discussion Questions:
How does today's culture (in movies, music, etc) define love?

How do your friends define love?

If your best friend came to you and asked this question: "How do I know when I'm in love with someone?" what would you say?

Do you believe that you choose to fall in love, that it just happens to you, or some combination? Explain.

Why could it be dangerous to base your love solely on feelings?

Christian spends a lot of time discussing the fact that love is an action. Have you ever seen people who say they are in love, but do not act that way towards each other? How did it make you feel? Do you think they really are in love? Why or why not?

This chapter lists some "actions" of love. What are some actions that you would use to describe how love should be shown to each other?

When Christian discusses love being a sacrifice he also addresses the issue of boundaries – where sacrifice can go too far. What boundaries do you think are appropriate for a relationship? What things are "out of bounds" and should never be tolerated in a relationship? How can you protect yourself from those kinds of actions? Have you ever seen anyone else in that kind of situation? What did you do?

How do I know if I've found the one?

Six ways to be sure

"How do I know if this is the one?" I cannot tell you how many times I have heard this, or been asked this question. It is a good question I believe, and one that must be asked and answered with honesty (sometimes brutal), objectivity, and wisdom. If you are planning on moving into a very serious level of relationship, one where you are talking about engagement and marriage, I think you must be able to truly answer this question.

Before I met Mandy, I used to talk about how I could not wait to find my wife. I used to be so confident that I would know exactly who she was when I met her, and that I would know exactly how to treat her, and how to be the most romantic person ever (I struggle with prideful aspirations sometimes!). The winter of my freshmen year of college we began to spend time together very regularly. As we moved through the friendship, and then into committed dating, we eventually came to a point where we began to wonder—is this it? Have we found each other? Is this for life? Much to my ego's surprise, when I began to confront these questions, I soon saw much of what I understood fall apart.

As I began to seek God for whether Mandy was "the one" (I asked God this question literally every night for over six months) I unknowingly launched myself into one of the hardest times of my life. The struggle for healing is discussed in a previous chapter, what I want to talk about in this chapter is what I learned through this process. It is important to note, that before I began this process I was totally in love with Mandy—who she was, and who we were together. Although this was true, I learned that making this decision involved far more than just being in love. In this chapter I will discuss three dangers that hinder your ability to make a wise decision, and then several tools that I have found incredibly helpful.

Hindrances to Hearing God

#1) Responding To Pressure Rather Than God

One of the most important ingredients to finding God's heart for you on this, is to not be under any pressure from anyone. As you know by now, this book is written in part to combat the pressure put on young Christians by the popular Christian culture. So, of course, we need to be aware and objective about that. But pressure can come from a number of different places.

In my friendship circle about half of my friends married before they were 22. That is young! Because of this, there has been a pressure created in my sub-culture of young adult friends to marry young. It is crazy to hear some of my single friends talk about how this has affected them. They talk about how they feel if they do not find someone soon, then they will never find someone. Many times I find them struggling with loneliness and sometimes even despair. But so much of this has been created by the culture around them—an unseen and unwarranted pressure to marry young! We have talked about seeing this for what it is and not allowing it to affect them. In your life, are there pressures from the people you hang out with? From the crowd or sub-culture that you associate with? And if so, how has it affected how you feel about yourself and your future?

I think pressure (although I have never personally experienced this) can also come from parents, loved ones, "the way our family always does it," or even the secular culture. But in relationships I have observed, what I have seen to be the worst kind of pressure is the one that is levied by your partner. I have seen many cases where one person in a relationship becomes "sure" of the future of the relationship before the other one does. This can be very dangerous. When pressure is brought to bear in a committed relationship it very easily slips into manipulation and control, which are both very ungodly.

The pressure I am talking about manifests in several ways. For instance, one person in the relationship says something like, "I really feel like God has shown me that you are the one." Now on the surface that may look harmless, but unless the other person has also come to that conclusion, what it can do in their mind is remarkably dangerous. Even without intentional pressure, words like that can send your partner reeling because they begin to feel guilty for not feeling that way, or that they have missed God's will. Or they may go the other way and feel incredibly trapped by you, feeling that a decision that is rightfully theirs to make for their life has been usurped in some fashion.

In this situation, whoever feels the least amount of conviction or certainty must be allowed by the other partner to dictate the flow of the relationship, and the discussion. Let me explain. The worst thing that you can do to the person you love in this situation is to rush them. Remember, the first thing about true love—patience (1 Cor. 13:4). If you do rush them, what you will end up with is someone who is committing to you simply because they are responding to your pressure, and not because they truly want to. It is like holding a gun to someone's head and telling them to say "I love you." We talked about this at length in the chapter on emotional righteousness, and it is important to keep in mind while making this decision as well.

Because your partner loves you, you hold some power over them. That is just true—it is in the nature of love that we submit to one another, and that is the wonderful power of true love, but it can be wielded manipulatively if we are not careful. You see, many people, because they are in love with their partner, will not want to hurt their feelings. And that includes cases where being honest would hurt their feelings, so instead they will lie. One person may say, "I know you are the one, what do you think?" The other person is faced with a crucial decision if they are not sure yet— "Do I hurt the person I love a whole lot right now by being honest about my feelings, or do I hedge a little and say something like 'yeah I'm pretty sure too!' and let this be a whole romantic time!" So often I have seen people give into that pressure and say things they do not actually mean. When this happens, you are sowing bad seeds that will eventually reap hurt and destruction.

You may be thinking I spent way too long discussing this, but I think it is vital. The decision to choose your life partner must be made in an environment of peace, security, acceptance of feelings (whether easy to talk about or not) and love. We have to resist the urge to guilt trip each other ("I thought you said you loved me") and learn to respect each other's personal and unique journey to understanding God's will for our lives, even if this requires a good deal of patience.

#2) *Acting Married Before You Actually Are*

That leads me to my next foundational point for this section. We must understand that until you say, "I do," you and your partner are two distinct people. When you get married you will be joined as 'one,' but not before. I have seen many dating couples who act as if they are already 'one,' and that is not healthy for making this life decision. As you fall in love and then progress through being romantic and excited about where your lives are going together, it is very easy to begin to think as if your lives are already joined—but they truly are not. It is true that as you get closer and begin to commit more and more to each other, the Lord prepares your hearts for this, but there is a danger in thinking and acting in this vein.

I once had a couple tell me that they were praying together about whether God wanted them to get married. The girl from the relationship emailed me later saying that she still had doubts on her own, but when she prayed with her boyfriend she felt great about it. Please understand, I think it is important to pray together about this decision, but what I told this girl was that it is more important for each of you to pray alone. It is common-sense: when you pray together you both are certainly able to hear God's voice, but what else is coming into play? When you are together there is this "magic feeling," right? These wonderful love feelings. Do you think they can in any way hinder your ability to hear God? Absolutely. It is important to realize that you alone will make the decision to give your life to this person. Until you are married, you are single—and you are responsible for your life and the decisions of your life. The fact that the person you are dating feels peace about getting married is wonderful, but ultimately has nothing to do with your decision. That must come from you alone.

This is so important, I cannot stress it enough: if you marry because someone else thinks you should, or because you felt good when the two of you were praying together, you are asking for trouble. In marriage, hard times will come, and the way to get through those times is to know this fact: I made this decision. I chose to love this person no matter what comes in life. You do not want to be married and realize you never felt, in and of yourself, good about this. You must seek God and know on your own. You need to make the decision for yourself, independent from the other person. Your life is yours to give, and yours only.

#3) Being Caught In Romantic Bliss Rather Than Real Life
Another danger I believe we must be aware of is the power of romance. Most relationships have a "romantic high" for a number of months before real life sets in. During the romantic high the person you are in love with can seemingly do no wrong. They are the most beautiful, most perfect, most charming, most thoughtful, most amazing person ever created. What a find! This, however, is not real life. And when you get married you will not forever be on a romantic high. Most of marriage is going through life together, doing the normal real-life things like grocery shopping, cleaning, paying bills, raising kids, and so on. I am not saying marriage is not wonderful and amazing: it is, and I am madly in love with Mandy more now then ever. But the point is this: it is dangerous to make a life-long decision based on an unrealistic experience. And while the romantic-high "stage" of a relationship is wonderful, in truth it is very unrealistic. It is not real life.

I am a big proponent, then, for spending tons of time together in a variety of settings. Spend time alone, with friends, with the friends of one partner and the friends of the other, and with each partner's parents. Do a multitude of different activities too—go out to eat, to the movies, to a coffee shop, to your parents' house, to a soccer game . . . .The reason for me saying all this is that I want you to experience each other fully. You need to purposefully put yourselves into diverse situations in order to learn fully about one another. You may go out with your partner and his friends, and things might be great—but then if he comes with you and your friends— watch out! He is a totally different person, becoming overly jealous and grossly affectionate, obviously insecure about the relationship and trying to keep your attention. You never could discover that side of him though, without trying new venues. Let me try to explain this better.

It is easy, for a time, to give a wonderful impression to the person you are "falling in love with" every time you see her. For the first few months with Mandy, I was amazing. I never was in a bad mood, I never got angry with her, I never argued, I never hurt her feelings, I never looked or smelled anything but my absolute best—do you see what I am getting at? It takes time to be real with each other. You have to be patient and allow each other's true colors to come out. Because if you are going to get married, that is the person you will see every morning when you wake up, when you come home from work, when you go to bed. You will not see the amazing, no-fault, good-smelling person all the time, but you will see the real person every day. Some of you might think that makes marriage sound boring, but actually I think this is maybe the coolest thing about marriage, knowing you are getting the chance to spend your entire life with each other and not just certain special times.

Marriage for me was a decision to love Mandy, strengths and weaknesses, triumphs and failures, good and bad. I fell in love with and chose to love everything about her. Mandy and I have this joke we play with each other sometimes when one of us is complaining about the other person. For instance she might say for the millionth time that month how astoundingly loud I chew my cereal in the morning, and how it is probably waking up neighboring cities and countries. And I will say to her—"I bet you'll miss that when I'm dead!" Morbid joke I know, but it is true, and inevitably she will say—"Don't say that! I don't want to think about that— that's awful! I would miss it so much!" The point is this: We love each other through and through, real life and romantic bliss.

In order to know if this person is the one for you, my advice is this: get into real life. Many things can stand in the way of this. For some it is availability. You can only see each other on the weekends, or you can never see each other for more than 3 hours at a time. That is not enough time to experience real life. For some it is distance. You live far away from each other and you talk on the phone everyday and visit once a month, but that just is not a good test for marriage. For some it is simply allowing enough time to get over the initial powerful infatuation and lovey-dovey feelings. I am not saying any of these are bad, but I am saying take your time. Do not make your decision during these situations, but wait. Wait until you have experienced real life. And I would say, do not just live one month of real life and say, "OK, that's it—we know it's right!" It takes time for real life to happen. You need to be around each other when hard times come in life, and when great times come. You need to be around each other when nothing is happening at all. And it is impossible to manufacture this stuff, so the only answer is time. Just be together and allow life to happen.

The last three topics I have discussed form an environment of peace; freedom of your will from outside pressure, manipulation, or control; and a true and real testing ground of a relationship. I believe a more healthy decision can be made in this environment than in others full of pressure and false ideals about each other. From within this environment I have several pieces of advice to discuss that have helped me tremendously in making the major decisions of my life—college, marriage, and career. I want to share these with you in this next section.

Six Tools To Make A Wise Decision:

Seek God's Direction And Listen To His Voice
This should be obvious for most of us, however it is so fundamentally and foundationally important that it must be said. In all of our life, no matter what situation or decision, we should be seeking God for his input, direction, leading, and guidance. We should be seeking both God's Word for answers and leading, and the Holy Spirit's leading in our hearts. Concerning marriage, as we've already discussed, God's Word clearly tells us that we should be seeking to marry a Christian. Beyond that though, we need to give total attention to the Holy Spirit leading us in this decision.

The Lord promises in Matthew 7:7, "ask and it will be given to you; seek, and you will find; knock and it will be opened to you." God has direction for you. Jeremiah 29:11 tells us that God has plans for a good future for you. So in every decision in life, and especially in one as monumental and life-altering as marriage, we must begin by seeking the face of God. At the outset of my relationship with Mandy I committed it to the Lord and asked God to lead me and direct me. I wanted, and still want, God's will in my life totally with no compromise. Then when we began to talk more seriously, I again committed our discussions and my personal seeking to God.

In Proverbs 16:3 David instructs us to "commit your works to the Lord, and your thoughts will be established." This is exactly what we are seeking when we are asking God so show us direction about a potential spouse. I remember those days when I was mulling over the future of Mandy and myself. There were so many thoughts, so much different advice coming from so many different sources—what I needed, and what I waited for, was God to establish my thoughts. That word "establish" is so powerful. This is a place we must come to before we can truly enter into the covenant of marriage. Our thoughts, our intentions, our desires, our choice must be grounded, rooted, planted firmly in complete assurance in our hearts and from God. The importance of this is indescribable. We must come to the place where we know that we know that we know. We must come to a place of total faith.

The reason I am so firm in writing this is that when we fall in love, it is very easy to lose the ability to objectively hear God's leading in our lives. Why? Because our emotions and desires for this person are so strong, that they, in a sense, distort or paralyze our ability to hear God! For this reason, I am going to talk through several "checks and balances" that helped me to truly understand God's plan for my life. But the reason I began with "hearing the Lord's direction" is that ultimately, after everything else I will tell you, the decision comes down to you and what you feel the Lord is telling you.

I love Psalm 119:105—"Your word is a lamp to my feet, and a light to my path." This is what God's leading will be in your life if you truly submit to God and listen patiently for his leading. The Lord desires to shine His light upon the path of your life in every area, including this decision. And I believe that He will, as we are obedient and patient in waiting for His guidance. In reading these next few sections, keep in mind that God's light will shine more clearly as each of these tools is implemented.

Seek Wise Counsel

Proverbs 11:14 declares, "Where there is no counsel, the people fall; but in the multitude of counselors there is safety." I cannot tell you how important this principle of wise counsel is. In many ways, Mandy and I feel that it literally saved us from a horrible marriage.

When I was younger I thought about marriage a lot. I thought, for some reason, that I would get married by the time I was 18 and was always on the lookout for my wife from even the age of 14. I was so excited about finding her it felt like I could not wait. In the back of my mind, for some reason, I always had this idea that before I asked her to marry me, I would go to the elders of my church and ask their approval first. That may sound strange, but it stuck with me, and that is what I did.

Mandy and I came to a point in our relationship where we were seriously considering engagement. At the time Mandy felt more comfortable than I did, but I told her that I was ready, and we started to make some preliminary plans. I told her though, that before anything could happen, I needed to talk to the elders. So one day, I set up a meeting with the elders of my church and my dad. I sat them down and told them how much I loved Mandy and how we were talking about engagement, but that I knew it was a huge decision, and I wanted their wisdom and guidance. They prayed with me and then one by one began to list concerns they had: were we healed enough from some stuff in our pasts? was Mandy truly ready to marry someone who would work in ministry his whole life? was I ready to make the commitment and lose some of the freedom that singleness allows? . . . and then the big one. They asked me, "Do you really want to get engaged? Are you ready?" I faltered.

As the night went on they proceeded to say that they stood behind me, but that they had their reservations, and they would feel better if we waited for several months and both individually got some counseling. This was devastating!! I was so upset—not because I disagreed with them, but because I knew I would have to tell Mandy.

For some reason, because of my immaturity, I never was totally honest with Mandy concerning my numerous fears about marriage and commitment. It got so bad at one point that I had lost all peace in my heart, and was beginning to feel like an emotional wreck. But I did not tell this to Mandy for fear of hurting her—or worse, losing her.

After the meeting with the elders, I still was not totally honest with her, and I basically said they wanted us to wait for a while. Not too long after, another couple to whom we had decided to make ourselves accountable called us and asked us to come over. I ended up going out to get some stuff with the husband, while Mandy stayed and talked for hours with the wife. She shared with Mandy several horrible dreams she had about us getting married, while the husband shared with me his insights—he called me on the fact that I was not being honest with Mandy, and told me that I would regret this the rest of my life if I based my marriage on a lie.

Needless to say this all turned our world completely upside down. As I came clean with Mandy, we went from talking engagement, to not even knowing if we loved each other. There were tears and anger and despair . . .God had gotten our attention.

I later heard a tape by a man named Derrick Prince. He spoke of how he had made himself accountable to 15 people—and that he vowed not to marry the woman he loved until all 15 had come into agreement. After seeing how misguided I had become on my own (and notice, I consider myself able to hear God pretty well!) Mandy and I agreed to slow down, give the relationship totally over to God again, get into counseling, and enlist a group of people who would have to "agree" for us to ever get engaged. After several months, the Lord gave me the best gift of my life . . . He brought Mandy and I into the most wonderful and loving relationship, more than I could have ever asked for. But even as my feelings became stronger, and my doubts disappeared, many of the people I was accountable to did not feel free to say they would agree with us moving forward.

It took time, but eventually one by one, each person came to me and said they felt good about us being married. Once this was done, the ball again was in my court, and this I must stress again. Even after these people whom I trusted explicitly gave me their approval, the decision was still ultimately mine to make. And I chose wisely!

One of the greatest pieces of advice that I can give in this book is this: surround yourself with people you trust to speak into your life and into your relationship. These are not just "anybodies"—I am talking about people who are willing to pray for you on a regular basis, people who will invest in getting to know your potential spouse, and people who are truly invested over time in your life. These people will often include your parents, your friends, trusted mature members of your church whose marriages you respect, trusted mature single people in the church who are invested in your life, and leaders who have authority and wisdom in your life. Find these people, and listen to them. Some couples I know have enlisted "mentoring couples" to help them through dating. This is a great way to have people speaking into your relationship on a regular basis.

One of the hardest things to do in life is to submit when it is not what you want to do. I take no pride in what we were able to do, I believe it was fully God's grace that we were able to humble ourselves and submit. But remember this, "God resists the proud, but gives grace to the humble" (1 Peter 5:5). If you are above God and his leading and rebuke, he will resist you. "Therefore, humble yourselves under the mighty hand of God, that He may exalt you in due time" (1 Peter 5:6). I know that God saved us. He saved us from starting a marriage under the most unhealthy and ungodly premises. And because of several people who loved us enough to be brutally honest with us, we had the glory of being humbled under the mighty hand of God. And in due time, he did lift us up.

So I encourage you to be humble. Seek wise counsel and be accountable not just with words, but also with action. Many people give "lip service" to being accountable in their life. It sounds great, until you get counsel that is hard to follow. It is easy to say you want to do this, but it is difficult to actually live it. People can rationalize away wise counsel because they do not want to hurt each other, or they do not want to be inconvenienced in their plans. Another reason this can be so difficult is that sometimes things will still turn out OK even if you don't follow the advice. What this advice can do though, is take you from having something that is good, to having something that is the best. Mandy and I could have gotten married and ignored the elders and our friends. I am confident God would still have blessed our marriage. But I am also confident that our marriage, at least in the beginning, would have been much more difficult. And at some point we would have needed to go through that breaking and healing process to ever have a healthy relationship. By truly being accountable we were given the gift of a healthier marriage, the best God had for us, instead of just something good.

As you go through this, do not be in a hurry, but allow God in due time to lead you into his will, which may or may not be with the person whom you are currently with. I know that is scary for someone who is reading this right now but feeling like they love the person they are with. Remember though, that in 1 Peter it says for us to cast "all your care upon Him, for He cares for you (1 Peter 5:7). We must learn to trust God even when it might not make a whole lot of sense. God wants the BEST for you, and if you follow Him, I firmly believe that He will lead you.

Use Your God-Given Wisdom

This is an asset that can be overlooked, in my experience, by many with more "charismatic" beliefs. I can say this because I would place myself in that group as well. A strong point of many in those types of churches is their zeal and ability to listen to God's leading and direction. Unfortunately, for some, if I were to mention the importance of using our mind in this decision, they would feel I was belittling the importance of hearing God's voice and that simply is not true!

I have even seen people take Proverbs 3:5, which instructs us to "lean not on your own understanding" and make that to mean that when we are deciding on our spouse, we need only to listen to God's voice, not our understanding. In fact, some would argue, your understanding may often be opposed to God's voice, and you need to forsake your understanding, and listen to God.

Now, I believe this to a point and for certain situations. I believe, for instance, when confronted with an evangelistic situation, where our carnal mind is holding us back from being bold, we need to forsake what is "normal" and take a risk—trusting God. However, it would be ludicrous for me to tell you to totally forsake any and all mental capacity as you begin to speak to this person, and hope that the Holy Spirit takes hold of your mouth and begins to move it, right?

The point is this, Proverbs 3:5 tells us first to "Trust in the Lord with all your heart." I believe that God has given us our minds, as well as His Voice for leading. Romans 12:2 tells us that our minds are being transformed so that we can "test and approve what God's will is—His good, pleasing, and perfect will." That verse speaks directly to what we are seeking in the situation of choosing a lifelong mate—God's will! God has given us a mind. God has given us understanding. God has commanded us to seek wisdom (Prov. 4:5) and promised us he would provide it amply (James 1:5). So when we use this gift from God, we are in fact trusting in the Lord!

My basic argument is this: For such a huge decision, we need to employ every tool the Lord has prepared for us in seeking and testing his will for our life.

How does this discussion apply practically to your relationship? When you come to the place where you are serious enough to be thinking about engagement and marriage, and you are trying to seek God's will for your life, do not be afraid to sit back and use your mind to analyze your relationship. Ask yourself questions—"Does she challenge me?" "Does he bring out the best in me?" "Do I feel I can be myself totally when I am with her?" "Will our individual plans and dreams for the future be able to work out together?" Essentially you are asking—"Does this make sense?"

Understand that much of the argument of my book is the importance of spending time in a committed relationship before making the decision to spend your lives together. Therefore, after spending time together in this relationship, you both individually should be at a place where you can objectively analyze where you are and where you could be going. If this person is the one you are going to marry, then your mind and God's voice will line up together. Try to avoid the stigma that exists in much of Christianity today for plain old critical thinking. Think of it this way: if you can create serious doubts just by analyzing the relationship (essentially a mock furnace), what will happen when two years into marriage you are faced with some serious difficulties or struggles (the real furnace). What doubts will arise then?

Only Time Will Tell

In some ways I already addressed this issue when I talked about "real life," but it is worth re-visiting it in this section. Time is very powerful. I have found that as a test, time can solidify or destabilize many ideas or feelings that initially were "definite." That is why there is a principle in the Bible of waiting to see and waiting to grow. Unfortunately I cannot give a formula for how long these processes take. I think for every person and every couple it can be different. But there are some definite principles here that we can discuss that can guide anyone.

Psalm 40:1 says "I waited patiently for the Lord, he turned to me, and heard my cry." There are times in life, and in the Bible, where the Lord holds his word until the appointed time, until the right time. In your life, you may find a desire, a longing inside, to make a decision now. You may find yourself even becoming agitated with the Lord that he does not speak to you right away, that everything has not come together yet. I would encourage you to wait patiently for the Lord, and continue to cry to him. If the Lord is holding onto his answer there is a reason.

One night I was tired of asking God if Mandy and I were supposed to get married, so I drove out to my parent's old house (we had sold it, and no one lived there yet, so it was empty) with my guitar and Bible. I sat in my old living room and set my heart towards God—"I am not leaving until you give me an answer!!!" Ever say anything like that before? Well, I was not very good at playing the guitar so it was not very long before that became frustrating, and reading the Bible was not seeming to help either. So being the very holy fervent man of God that I am—after about 10 minutes (maybe!) I slumped to my knees and said—"God! Why is this so hard! I have waited and prayed every night for 3 years for a wife. Now I am in love, and you refuse to lead me!!" Immediately God spoke to my heart.

He showed me how much work needed to be done in me, personally, before I could even begin to hear his voice on that question. This was one of two crucial moments in my journey to knowing God's will in this area of my life. And the point is this: I had been praying and seeking counsel and following all my guidelines for a long time up to this point. I could have just decided to go forward even though my thoughts were not totally established yet. But I waited. Waiting is so hard sometimes, especially when you are in love, but it is so powerful. Because I waited, God "inclined to me, and heard my cry."

James 1:4 teaches us more about this lesson:

But let patience have its perfect work, that you may be perfect and complete, lacking nothing" (NKJV).

Perseverance must finish its work so that you may be mature and complete, not lacking anything (NIV).

Remember how I said that time was powerful? One of the powerful aspects of time is its ability to allow us to see deeper levels of our partners and ourselves. I have heard it said many times in counseling situations that the human heart is like an onion (gross huh?), and that as time continues, if we submit our heart to the Lord, he will peel back layer after layer exposing deeper and deeper levels of healing, maturity, pruning, and growth that is needed in our lives. In order for patience to have its "perfect work" we will need time. Patience and perseverance by definition need time. It is easy to persevere for 30 seconds or even a year. But allow time to have its full work in you and in your relationship. See what time will turn up. Be patient, and allow your relationship and yourselves as individuals to grow to a place of maturity. I am not saying you need to be perfect to get married, but I am saying take your time. I have one other thought about time. Psalm 37:7 reads:

> Rest in the Lord, and wait patiently for Him; do not fret
> because of him who prospers in his way . . . (NKJV).

This may not be a big deal for you, but I think sometimes we can get caught up in others' lives and begin to covet what they have, and then in turn make poor decisions based on that covetousness. We see our friends having girlfriends, or wives, and we feel inside somehow betrayed by God. I know there was a time in my life where out of my four best friends, one was married, one was engaged, and two had great girlfriends (who eventually became their wives). I, on the other hand, was relegated to hanging out by myself, coming home early and watching TV, and praying every night for God to "bring my wife!" In the midst of that, it would have been easy for me to make rash decisions about dating, engagement, and even marriage. Making a decision about any of these for the wrong reasons will prove unsuccessful most of the time, and envy, or wanting to be like others, is a very wrong reason. So, as hard as it may seem I encourage you to "rest in the Lord." God has so much in store for you during this time of your life, right now. Although you might want someone to love more than you can describe, God wants you now. Allow God to work in your life, and be used by him. I dealt with this in another chapter in detail, but know that God has huge plans for your life while you are single. Do not miss them by lusting after the future.

To end this section, let me share a little story. I was sitting in my pastor's office one day, talking about the recent developments with Mandy and me. It was during the time where God had broken us, and we had no idea what was going to happen. And I asked him (because I used to ask everyone this question, so I could know when it happened to me)—"how will I know if she is the one?" And he said to be patient. "Over time," he said, "the two of you will either grow apart or grow together. You will just know." I took that to heart. I can still remember the hand gestures he used when he said that to me. And some time later, I just knew. After allowing time to pass, I came to realize that we had grown together more tightly than ever before. And I knew that I never wanted to be apart again.

The X-Factor

In some ways, what I am about to write will seem to go against everything I have written in this book thus far. The X-Factor test for knowing if you have found the one is difficult to describe by nature. It will be different for everyone, but it is always powerful. When I say X-Factor, I am referring to the feeling that this relationship is something different. Something special. Now remember, everyone has that feeling in the first parts of a relationship when romance is in your blood, and every single song you hear on the radio makes your heart jump. I am talking about something that still exists after a long time.

People talk about finding a "soul-mate." I used to not give much credence to this whole idea, but I think there is some truth in it now. When you know you have found the one, there is just this feeling that you have been looking for each other forever and finally found one another. Or, the feeling that the two of you just totally complete each other like no one you have ever met before. It is a burning desire, an intense passion for one another, like what Song of Solomon talks of. I know I spent a lot of time in this book down-talking the importance of romance and feelings. But in the end, these are crucial as well. The X-Factor is that undying romance, those feelings that consume your thoughts, flood your dreams, and make your heart beat when you see each other.

For me, I think the X-Factor became clear to me when I realized that I truly, truly did not want to live without Mandy for the rest of my life. I thought about growing old together, having kids together, buying a house together, doing ministry together, traveling together, etc. The thought of doing that with anyone else repulsed me. I knew that she was all that I wanted and needed.

Again, this is difficult to write about. I do not think you should base your whole decision on something as flimsy as an X-Factor, but at the same time, I have heard people try to talk themselves out of an X-Factor because some other areas do not line up. I have looked at some couples who are agonizing over their relationship and just thought to myself, "You've got it! You have what many people spend much of their lives hoping and looking for. You have found that special person. Why risk throwing it away? Go for it!"

Let me give you an example. Two of my greatest friends started dating when they were sophomores in high school. Even at an early age they could feel that this was something special. They graduated and got jobs . . . and then got engaged! Now to the wisdom of the world that sounds totally crazy! And in most cases I have to admit, I would counsel against this. But these two had that something special. They knew it, and everyone around them knew it. What is important is that they did not get engaged simply because of the X-Factor. All the other areas I outlined here lined up too: people were in agreement with them, they had heard from the Lord, etc. But I think many people would have said that there was no way for them to know. Some would argue that they needed to experience life, go to college, and get careers. But these two knew they had found something incredible, something they might never find again on this earth. So they were engaged and married when they were 18 years old! They have been married for six years now, have three amazing daughters, and are following God's call on their lives. They have been part of a ministry that has reached hundreds of young people, and now they are working to co-pastor a church.

The point of that story is that sometimes you just need to realize that what you have is special and worth fighting for. I told you that I like balance; I am warning you, it can get confusing. I wrote in the last chapter that you should not do drastic things like move to another state to follow your girlfriend right? Well, that is true . . . sometimes. But there must be balance! There comes a time when your relationship becomes so important, where you think finding the one is a pretty big deal, and maybe I should do something drastic. This is the X-Factor. Totally unpredictable, hard to write about, but very powerful.

To summarize myself: I am not saying you should lose your mind and follow your boyfriend of six months into the Amazon to see if you are meant for each other. I am saying two things: 1) Look for the X-Factor. Do you have it? Do you have that 'hard to describe but definitely there' feeling that this one is just right? 2) If you do, maybe it's worth fighting for so you don't lose it. That could mean doing something drastic like switching colleges. Or it could mean going to counseling and getting healed so the relationship can go further.

This is not the most important point in this chapter. In fact, I considered leaving it out because I so strongly do not want to mislead people. But I would not be totally honest if I did not include this. I think this is one part of the whole picture. And I urge you to pray about what this means to your relationship.

God's Peace—"Let The Peace Of Christ Rule In Your Hearts" (Col. 3:15)

I know I have said this about several of my earlier points, but this truly is perhaps one of the greatest tests of God's will in my life. Peace is so enormously important, and yet the difficult part is that it is completely unscientific. It is so subjective, and totally immeasurable by any outside source, that it can often be very difficult to gauge honestly. Personally, when I know that I do not have peace about something, but I still want to go forward with it, I begin to rationalize the "lack of peace" away—"it must have been something I ate" or quote scripture like "God gives me the desires of my heart." Have you ever tried that? And all the while, God is speaking to me, but I am afraid to listen.

Sometimes I think "peace" is almost the last line of defense for God. If you will not listen to others, if you will not objectively see the telltale signs in your relationship, if you are in a hurry and will not wait to see how things shake out, then God is forced to take away your peace. Jesus' peace is a gift that he left for us, because he knew this world would be full of tribulation, trials, and stress (John 14:27; 16:33). But it is also a test. I believe that when we are abiding in Christ, only then does his peace truly "rule in our hearts" (Colossians 3:15). If we are living in sin it certainly does not, and if we are sliding out of God's will it will not either. It is amazing how much God loves us. I used to be afraid that I would miss God's will, but I realized that, if I continued to submit my heart to him in honesty, he would never let me slip that far!

Another way to look at this idea of peace is to look at faith vs. doubt. Romans 14:23 tells us that, "everything that does not come from faith is sin." And James 1:6-7 declares,

> He who doubts is like a wave of the sea, blown and tossed by the wind. That man should not think he will receive anything from the Lord; he is a double-minded man, unstable in all he does.

I know those Scriptures sound a little harsh, but the truth here is crucial. When I talk about having a "lack of peace" it is equivalent to saying you are having a "lack of faith" or that you are in doubt about God's will in your relationship. If you are honest with yourself, and find that you are in this place, God's Word is clear. It says that to move forward and ignore the lack of faith (or peace, which is a lack of a faith) would not only be sinful, but also that God would not bless it and it would most likely fail.

We need to listen to our peace. If you are in a relationship and you know deep inside that you do not have peace, then you need to make the difficult step of dealing with that. Look at it objectively. How do we become objective? Sometimes it helps to ask yourself, "What would you tell someone else if they came to you asking advice for the same situation you are in?" (I give credit again to my pastor for leading me through this as well!) Would you tell them to back off? To wait? To seek counsel? To go forward? It can be hard to be objective sometimes, but we need to honestly deal with our deepest feelings, instead of hiding from them.

Follow your peace. I know that when I finally asked Mandy to marry me, I would actually try to make myself feel a lack of God's peace. I would think about statements like, "You will have to be with this person FOREVER!!!! You will be trapped!!" I would honestly try to scare myself (I have some very odd idiosyncrasies, I know) and I could not. My peace was solid. It was built on the rock of God's leading and his will, and not on the sand of my own ideas and wishes.

I want to end by looking at Philippians 4:6-7 in several pieces.

Do not be anxious about anything—This is great. It is hard to truly do this when faced with such an important decision. In the end remember how much God loves you. Remember that Jeremiah 29:11 tells us that God has good plans for you. God is faithful. He keeps his word. His love for you is undying. He wants what is best for you more than you do. He will lead you and guide you. He will take you into a great place. You can trust him completely because he has your best interests in mind, and he loves you with a perfect love, so there is truly no reason to be anxious.

but in everything, by prayer and petition, with thanksgiving, present your requests to God—This is what we are talking about. Take your relationship, with your hopes and dreams and worries and doubts, and lay them before your Father. Remember how we began this whole section: "he who seeks will find?" It is simple right? "Let your requests be made known to God" is so simple. Be honest with God, and tell him everything! He is listening to your prayer.

And the peace of God, which transcends [NJKV— "surpasses"] all understanding—Sometimes God's peace will astound you. Even when in your mind it seems impossible or too difficult, God can surpass our understanding!

will guard your hearts and your minds in Christ Jesus.—This is my prayer for you. That the peace of God would indeed be a guard, a strong protection, and a shield for your heart and your mind! Listen to your peace. It will guard you from giving your heart away too quickly, or to the wrong person. It will guard your mind from being confused or deceived. God's peace is a powerful defense as we search for God's will.

Lead Me Lord . . .

As I said earlier, after all of this advice, in the end the decision is ultimately yours. No one can, nor should, make this decision for you. This is such an important decision for the both of you, take everything and ponder it in your heart and trust God to lead you. Some people "know" right away, and others take years. Be patient with yourself and your partner. Allow yourselves to be who you are, and to discover this in the right time, be it quickly or not so quickly. Also, I know that hearing all this advice may be overwhelming. I do not want to create any sense of, "there is no way I will ever be able to check all of that stuff!" Everyone is different, and for me when I have to make very important decisions, I like to gather information from the four corners of the earth, weigh it all before God and in my heart, and then make a decision when I feel total peace. Other people might not be like that, but my two major goals in this process are 1) getting objectivity instead of having your head in the clouds, and 2) having peace instead of doubt.

However you want to do it, you need to look at yourself, your relationship, and how you look in your relationship, through someone else's eyes—that is objectivity. Your parents, your friends, your pastors—any of these may see problems or raise questions that need to be dealt with before you get married or even engaged. And secondly, to go into marriage with doubt is truly equivalent to shooting yourself in the foot and then trying to run across the U.S. Anything (especially marriage) based in doubt, as we discussed earlier, will fail. You must have peace. Because trials will come and in those trials, your relationship and you personally in the relationship must be built on the rock. Jesus told these parables for a reason—they are truth. So do not be hasty and make sure you are not "double-minded" and "unstable in all" you do (James 1:8).

Those last two paragraphs may have sounded a little harsh, but they are meant to put a little of the fear of God into you, because this is such a major step in life. However, there is no need to be afraid or anxious of making a wrong decision if you are truly submitted to God. Let me end this chapter with a Psalm that has always been a stalwart for me in decisions like this. It is good to remember God's love and kindness for us!

> To you, O Lord, I lift up my soul. O my God, I trust in You,
> let me not be ashamed . . . Show my your ways, O Lord;
> teach my your paths. Lead me in Your truth and teach me,
> for You are the God of my salvation; on You I wait all the
> day. Remember, O Lord, Your tender mercies and Your
> loving kindnesses, for they are from of old. Do not remember
> the sins of my youth, nor my transgressions; according to
> Your mercy remember me, for Your goodness' sake, O Lord
> (Psalm 25:1-7, NKJV).

Small Group Discussion Questions:
Have you ever experienced your emotions getting in the way of your ability to hear God's voice clearly? What did you do?

How would it make you feel to ask some people you respect to pray about whether you and your girlfriend/boyfriend should get married? Would you be afraid of their response? What if they said they did not feel good about it, what would you do then?

Take a second to list a few people whom you could ask to come into agreement with you before you got married.

How long do you think a couple should be together before they make a decision about marriage? If it is a "distance relationship" do you think it is important that they spend a certain amount of time living in close proximity to each other?

How important do you think the "X-factor" is? Can you describe the "X-factor" in your own words? Do you believe in "soul-mates?" If so, what does that mean?

When you think of making the decision to choose one person for the rest of your life, how does it make you feel? Do you feel nervous? Scared? Excited? Something else?

Of the six methods used to make this decision, which ones are most helpful to you and why? Are there any others that you personally would add to that list?

Conclusion

Final thoughts:
Trusting God for your future

After everything that I have written, I want to reiterate the centrality of Jesus in this process. From the beginning, when you are simply forming an idea of what you are looking for in a mate, to the end, when you have found him or her, Jesus needs to be central. You can read thousands of books on dating, and glean all sorts of great ideas, but in the end the decisions still fall to you alone. You alone decide whether you think dating is ok. You alone decide the boundaries within your relationships. And you alone decide whether to get married or not. And because of that, it is vital to be seeking Jesus in all of these steps.

This actually speaks to the reason I wrote this book in the first place. As I mentioned earlier, I have spent some time traveling and meeting young people in different parts of the nation. My increasing feeling is that many are feeling a lack of direction from the Christian culture of our day—except the advice of not dating at all. While this advice may serve to prevent some sin, I believe it actually leaves many people at a loss for how to move forward in this area of their life.

I have a great desire to see that change. I hope that you can take some tools from this book to help you make godly and healthy decisions about dating and marriage. But mostly what I hope is that this book points you to Jesus. I truly desire for 1) your relationship with Christ to grow as a result of reading this book, and 2) for you to be able to make Jesus the center around which your relationship is built, wherever it may go.

Pressure to Marry Young

I want to close by addressing three issues briefly. First, I want to comment on the pressure that exists in some people's lives to marry young. I know many people who fear that if they do not find their spouse while they are young, then they will be never find anyone, and will be lonely forever. This is not true. While it seems true that often it is easier to find someone while you are younger, God is bigger than that. I have a good friend who had wanted to be married in his early twenties, but was nearing 30 and had yet to find anyone. Then one day, she walked into church! As soon as they began to date, they had a feeling this was it. Now they are married. That story is such a testimony to God's faithfulness. This man was single because he was following God's plan for his life—and in the end God rewarded him.

Try not to be pushed by any pressure to marry by a certain age. Even if your friends are all getting married, it does not mean that you are missing the boat if no one is in your life. Proverbs speaks a lot about the woes of being married to someone who is not good for you. I believe it is much better to be single than to be married to someone with whom you will not be happy. I know that for people who long to be married, this time in life can be lonely and frustrating. But it is important how you use this time. Remember to redeem the time of being single by enjoying it completely, and serving the Lord without distractions.

Unafraid to Break Up

Along those same lines, if you are in a relationship and you honestly feel that it should end, but you don't want to end it because you do not want to be alone, be bold and end it. I know breaking up is difficult. I know that sometimes you begin to think you will never find anyone else, but you have to remember the principles we talked about in this book already. God has a plan for your life. He has a good and perfect gift for you. You can trust Him!

In the chapter about what to look for in a relationship, I used the verses about knowing a tree by its fruit. Conversely, you can know a tree by the absence of its fruit too. In Matthew 21, Jesus approaches a fig tree hoping to find some fruit to eat. Instead he only sees leaves. I have read in a commentary somewhere that since it had leaves on it, Jesus presumed it would also have fruit. Leaves should be a sign that fruit is there as well. When he found no fruit, he cursed the tree and it withered. Apply this to a relationship. You may be in a relationship that looks good (has leaves) but in reality it is not bearing any fruit. You need to have the courage to allow it to die, if it is not producing fruit. God talks a lot in the Scriptures about how seeds have to die before they can live and bear fruit. If you are faithful to allow a fruitless relationship to die, God will be faithful to bring a fruitful one to you in His timing.

Biggest Decision of Your Life

The last point that I want to make in this book is that marriage is the biggest decision you will ever make aside from accepting Jesus as your Savior and Lord. I know I have said this already, but I want to leave you with this. This is the only decision in your life, besides becoming a Christian, where your spirit actually is joined to another. The Bible says that when you get saved your spirit is joined to God's. It also says that when you get married the two of you will become one. Think about that. It is not something to be taken lightly. Think about who you want to be in your life. Think about who God has called you to be. Think about your future, your plans, and your dreams. Think about how you want your kids to be—who you want your kid's mom or dad to be! This is the person you marry. He or she will be a part of every area of your life.

There is no decision so encompassing, so consuming, so future-of-your-life-altering, as this one. That is the main reason I felt the need to write this book. So many of my peers are trying to make this decision without any good help from the church. They are trying to decide with whom to join the rest of their future under the pressure of a Christian culture who says only date one person, then marry that person, and if you break up —then you just cheated on your eventual spouse! To make this monumental decision we need direction and understanding from the church. We also need an environment of honesty, peace, and the freedom to make mistakes without being condemned.

In closing then, I hope that this book has done some of that for you. I hope that you can feel a greater peace in dating, knowing that it truly is not a sin. I hope that you can learn to date in a godly and beneficial way, being allowed to enjoy relationship, and the process of getting to know each other, without the weighty pressure of always trying to figure out if "this is the one!" I pray that the advice in here will help you to steer clear of sin, both physical and emotional, that can happen in relationships. I know that dating relationships can be holy, can be edifying, and can be growing experiences. I know that God can lead, and will lead, a dating couple. I also hope that some of the practical advice in here will help you to be able to make that final decision when the day comes.

Let me leave you with a verse that dominates my life:

God has said, 'Never will I leave you; never will I forsake you' (Hebrews 13:5).

The power of that verse is that God is always with you. No matter what level of loneliness, or confusion, or frustration you might be feeling in your life, God is with you. And what is even better is that God will never turn his back on you. He will always be there when you call to Him. Throughout this whole process of finding someone with whom to spend your life, know that God is faithful. And if you completely trust him with this decision, then something good and perfect will happen in your life. You can trust Him. He will not let you down. Because God is good; he loves you; he wants the best for you; and if you will follow, he promises to lead you into life.

Works Cited

Belleville, Linda L. Women Leaders and The Church: Three Crucial Questions.
Grand Rapids, MI: Baker Books, 2000.

Bilezikian, Gilbert. Beyond Sex Roles: What The Bible Says About a Women's
Place in Church and Family. Grand Rapids, MI: Baker Books, 1993.

Groothuis, Rebecca Merrill. Good News for Women: A Biblical Picture of
Gender Equality. Grand Rapids, MI: Baker Books, 1996.

Keener, Craig S. Paul, Women, and Wives: Marriage and Women's Ministry in
the Letters of Paul. Peabody, Mass: Hendrickson Publishers, 1992.

es R., Jr. "A Tale of   Understanding the **Historical**
                                                        16:1

Did you like
"Finding the One?"

Want to tell your friends about it
or order more for your church or youth group?

Visit
www.christianjdunn.com
to order more copies.

If you would like to contact the author with comments, testimonies,
or for bulk orders, you can email him at:
cdunn@vcfbarn.com